When Grace Walked In

Amy Elizabeth

New Harbor Press
RAPID CITY, SD

Copyright © 2023 by Amy Elizabeth.

All rights reserved. No part of this publication may be reproduced, distributed or transmitted in any form or by any means, including photocopying, recording, or other electronic or mechanical methods, without the prior written permission of the publisher, except in the case of brief quotations embodied in critical reviews and certain other noncommercial uses permitted by copyright law. For permission requests, write to the publisher, addressed "Attention: Permissions Coordinator," at the address below.

Elizabeth/New Harbor Press
1601 Mt Rushmore Rd
Rapid City, SD 57701
www.NewHarborPress.com

Ordering Information:
Quantity sales. Special discounts are available on quantity purchases by corporations, associations, and others. For details, contact the "Special Sales Department" at the address above.

When Grace Walked In / Elizabeth. -- 1st ed.
ISBN 978-1-63357-288-1

1

THE MORNING LIGHT snaked its way across the grounds at the Hyatt mansion. The marble pillars were bathed in its amber glow and the sunlight gave the large oak doors a red hue. One slid noiselessly on its hinges. A sixteen-year-old shuffled out. His blond hair fell over his ears and his green eyes. He was a half foot shorter than the six-foot-tall bodyguard that closed the door behind them. His name was Connan.

He lived with his parents in a large mansion in the Rocky Mountains above Denver. His father, a security agent in the private sector, worked for a witness protection firm. It paid ridiculously well. Connan was escorted by his bodyguard to a waiting limo.

"Mr. Hyatt said you weren't allowed to stay at The Network all day." The red-headed bodyguard opened the back door. "I have a meeting at two, so we will head back after I am done."

Connan shouldered his backpack and ducked into the car. "Course he did . . ." He winced as he took his seat. He checked the bruise on his ribs. *At least Dad didn't break them. Nasty purple though, probably won't go away for another week!*

"He did ground you." The bodyguard slipped into the seat beside him.

"How could I forget, Daryn." Connan rolled his eyes. "He gave me a bruise so I wouldn't."

"You know very well he was just responding to the first punch . . . He shouldn't have hit you that hard."

Connan shook his head. "I was mad, he was mad . . . things got out of hand."

"He does care about you . . . in his own way." Daryn signaled to the driver to take off. "This is your last day with me, so try to be a good sport, aye?"

"I can't believe you're retiring . . ." Connan told him. "Is there anything I could say to keep you here? You're my only friend other than Hannah in that house."

"I'm almost forty, Connan," came the reply. "I was offered a higher-paying job and I couldn't pass it up. Besides, come Friday, I won't be needed anymore. Did you tell your dad you took the job at the Marine Academy?"

"That's what we fought about." Connan stared out his window. "He thinks I'm too young and should've asked him before accepting the job . . ." Connan sighed. "I thought he'd be happy since it was based out of my school."

"Maybe he just wanted to spend the summer with you?"

"You know he goes when the job calls."

Daryn leaned back in his seat. "He had plans to take you rock climbing next week and white water rafting after that . . . I'd be mad too if my kid took a job that was on the East Coast without telling me."

"And I'm sure he will cancel with the first call he gets. He always does, but I guess you're right . . . I'll apologize if he calls tonight."

"Good. Life is short, bud; too short to stay mad at people."

Connan stayed silent the rest of the trip into town. He wanted to tell his friend Alex all that had happened. Once Daryn had stepped out of the car, Connan jumped out and headed straight for the door of The Network. He said goodbye to his bodyguard with an "I'll see you after your meeting." He took out his Network pass and swiped it through the card lock. Only members were allowed during weekdays. An employee named Loyd welcomed him.

"Hi, Connan. Alex is set up in the gaming room waiting for you."

"Thanks, Loyd. If my bodyguard knocks on the door, come find me, would you?"

"Sure thing!" The day manager wrote himself a note to remember.

Connan made his way through the computer room to a large, windowless room with fifty-two-inch televisions lining the wall. A dark-skinned teen waved him down from a corner.

"Hey! Over here, Connan! Got 'Locked and Loaded' ready to go!"

Connan nodded to his friend and made his way around the couches. He put his pack down next to his friend and dug a controller out. He connected to the console and started customizing his character.

"So . . ." Alex's brown eyes flashed with excitement. "What happened? Don't leave me in suspense, bro!"

Connan raised his shirt. "This is how it went . . . He was furious."

Alex's jaw dropped. "Ouch! He did that? Dude, that's abuse!"

Connan shook his head. "More like self-defense . . . I threw the first punch."

"Oh . . . Is he going to let you go?"

"I tried to talk him into letting me, but after losing my temper . . . ."

"He said no."

"Yea, well, I'm kind of committed no matter what," Connan replied. "I already signed all the paperwork and sent it back to Sargent Tibbens. I can't back out unless dad calls Sarge himself."

They started their game. "I booked this room till noon," Alex said. "We can play then go eat and come back to the computer side."

"I'll have to leave around 2:30. Dad told Daryn I couldn't stay here all day."

"That's harsh, man."

"I did punch him . . . guess I deserve it." Connan laughed. "I'll smooth talk him later tonight if he calls."

Alex rolled his eyes. "If he calls . . . If he stayed any busier, he'd forget he had a son!"

They had two hours of playtime before they packed their things and went across the street to Cafe Bella. The June sun was perfect for them to sit outside on the patio. They ordered a couple cheeseburgers when the waitress came. Connan ducked as a couple stepped out onto the patio from inside the cafe.

"Great," he murmured. "Why is she here? It's like she doesn't care that anyone sees her!"

Alex turned his head to see who Connan was hiding from. "Dude, who's with your mom?"

Connan sank down even lower. "He's her Tuesday boyfriend so I call him Tuesday. He owns a barbershop on the outskirts of town."

"Dude . . ." Alex scratched at his dark head. "That's pretty bad, when they start openly flaunting their cheating ways . . . Does your dad know?" He tried to shield Connan from the couple's view.

Connan shook his head. "And it's a conversation I wouldn't dare enter without a ton of proof."

"But, you have a ton of proof . . . what happened to the pics from our recon mission?"

"Yea, well, I still think it will land me with a lot more bruises than I have now. Plus showing Dad those pics would be admitting that I snuck out."

"I see . . ." Alex looked at the couple again. "I mean, your mom is hot . . . just saying."

"Gross, man." Connan looked at his friend in disgust. "How could you?"

"What? She is for her age!"

"Can we just stop talking about her, please?" Connan sat up as the couple disappeared and the waitress brought out their meal.

Their conversation switched to what they would play on their computers and decided on a medieval survival game. They finished quickly and Alex paid with an "I'm paying this time, bro!" They went back across the street and logged in to the computer room. They found a secluded corner in the back of the room and set up their gear.

"Do you mind if I do something else?" Connan asked his friend.

"Depends on what you are doing instead of building our fortress with me . . . ."

"I want to finish the program I'm working on." Connan smiled.

"For sure! Do it, man! He needs to find out at some point. He needs to stop her from draining his accounts on her boyfriends! I'll play in solo mode!" Alex hunkered down behind his laptop screen.

Connan started working on the bug program he created to place on his dad's computer. It contained photo proof of all his mom's boyfriends. From Monday's mechanic to Friday's businessman, he had all the proof he needed. He would manually have to put it on his dad's computer so he wouldn't crash the laptop he used for work. Once Todd opened the file it would spam his entire screen with picture proof of his wife's lovers.

"It's about time he finds out." Connan couldn't help picture his dad's face when he found out his wife was cheating on him with five different men. Then, 2:30 came and went with no sign of Daryn. "Can I borrow your phone? Dad took mine, and I need to call Daryn."

"Sure, bro! May want to go out back, the manager isn't too happy when people take calls in here." Alex handed him his phone. "He says it's a place for gaming not for work . . . unless you're VIP."

"Thanks! I'll be right back." Connan got up and took his access card with him. He exited the front doors and went around to the alley. He started to dial Daryn's number.

"We pull this off and we'll be set for life! You can't back out now!"

Connan stopped at the sound of his bodyguard's voice. *Good, don't have to call him now.* Connan silently went to the end of the alley and peeked around the corner. *His meeting must have been longer than he thought it'd be. I'll wait for him to finish, then flag him down.*

"And what if we are discovered?" A stocky, shorter man spoke. "If Hyatt gets tipped off . . ."

Connan's heart rate rose. He instinctively turned on Alex's phone camera and started recording.

"He won't. He doesn't speak to his wife and he neglects to pay any attention to his kid. If anyone finds out we will kill them." Daryn paused. "I have access to his private hanger, as his son's bodyguard. That's our in. Once he lands, we take care of Jack and the pilot then Hyatt. He doesn't have a security detail and a bullet will take care of Jack. Hyatt is mine."

There was another pause then a third man spoke. "So, you get us into the airport. We take care of the pilot and the big guy while you take out Hyatt. After that we skip town and get our pay from Drummond and disappear to an island off the gulf."

"That sums everything up. I need to go get the kid now. He's probably looking for . . . ."

Connan stepped back and fumbled with his friend's phone. It had started to ring. Connan quickly declined the call and stuffed it in his belt as he ran back up the alley. *I won't make it out of the alley in time!* He stopped and turned around. He took the phone back out and started dialing Daryn's number again. He kept his head down as the three men rounded the corner.

"Connan?" Daryn did not look happy.

"Oh! Hey! Now I don't have to call you! You finish your meeting yet? If not I can go back inside." His hands shook.

"I'll call the car . . ." Daryn relaxed. "I'm guessing that's Alex's phone?"

"Yea, Dad took mine, remember?" Connan kept a casual look on his face. "So when you didn't show at 2:30, I asked Alex if I could call you on his." He sighed. "Turns out you were in the alley anyways . . ." Connan gave him an inquisitive look then looked at his friends. "A meeting in the alley? I figured you would have met your friends at a diner or something."

Daryn studied his face. "We met here so I could pick you up right after. Was there someone else in the alley?"

"No," Connan replied. "Just me. Alex's girl just tried to call but I declined it since I was trying to call you."

"Strange, that phone sounded a lot closer to the corner than you are now." Daryn eyed him.

"I didn't notice. Then again, I was about right here when your lot ran around the corner."

Daryn glared but kept his head. "Go get your stuff."

Connan shrugged his shoulders. "Alright. See ya at the front." He stuffed one of his hands in his pocket and turned on his heel. *I hope he bought it! He can read me like a book! Dad . . . He's going to kill Dad! I have to do something!* Connan could feel Daryn's eyes on the back of his head as he rounded the corner. He swiped back in as quickly as he could and went straight to his computer. He plugged his friend's phone into it and downloaded the video he recorded.

"Dude, you look whiter than usual, what's up?" Alex looked concerned. "You feeling okay?"

"Yea," Connan handed over the phone and closed his laptop. "Daryn was in the alley, scared me when he came around the corner with his friends! Anyway, he's waiting for me. I'll see ya later maybe."

"Y . . . Yea . . . see ya." Alex stared at his friend as Connan stuffed his laptop back into his pack and headed for the front door. He shook his head and went back to his game. Connan stuck his head back in the room. "Your girl called. She may be a little upset that I declined her call . . . May want to call her back." He disappeared into the lobby.

Please buy it, Daryn! Connan walked out the front doors of The Network. *Stay calm, Connan. Don't show fear!* "You ready?" He asked. Daryn did not look happy.

"Are you?" His bodyguard opened the door of the limo for him.

Connan shrugged. "I would've rather stayed till eight, but whatever." Connan ducked into the car and took his usual seat. *He doesn't seem suspicious. I'll talk to him as usual about my time with Alex and hopefully that keeps him at bay!* "I finished the virus I've been working on!"

"What did Alex say?" Daryn's voice was a bit shaky but Connan ignored it and started in.

"He thinks it's a genius way to tell Dad. We both agreed it's better than approaching him from the front! He'd kick my butt if I just blurted out that Mom had five boyfriends."

"Anything else interesting happen?"

Connan started in on their game of Locked and Loaded and the kids on the Internet that cussed them out and insisted they were cheating. "Course we don't cheat, we're just that good!" He told him about their zombie matches and making it to the higher levels before he went down on Alex. "That's about it, other than hiding from Mom when she and Tuesday walked out of the cafe. She's got some nerve!" Connan stared out the window for a few minutes before asking, "Want to spar this evening?"

Daryn had not completely relaxed. "Think you can take it with that massive bruise?"

"It's not that big . . ." Connan checked it again. "No, it's getting bigger . . . I really shouldn't have lost my temper. I know he can hit harder than me . . . ."

"Connan, I know you heard us back there." Daryn hissed. "You are a terrible liar."

Connan turned to him. "Why would I care, what you and your friends . . . I'm going to convince Dad to let me go to school. If he says no, I'll go anyway. I won't get in your way."

"How much did you hear?"

"Just you and your friends getting paid out by the mafia dude that's been all over the news. This Mafia dude going to raid the house or something?"

"Maybe it's best you leave and stay at school till you're eighteen." Daryn leaned toward him. "Just stay out of our way, Connan. I'd hate to have to involve you."

"Look, I said I was leaving tonight whether Dad agrees to let me go or not. At least the East Coast is safe and I won't be so . . . ."

"Alone . . . Connan, I can't back out of this. Drummond will kill me if I do, loose ends and all."

"I don't care about your stupid plans!" Connan pushed him away. "I just want to leave this place for good!"

2

CONNAN RETIRED TO his room while Daryn packed his things. *I can leave tonight for North Carolina... He doesn't want to involve me and I've convinced him I won't get in his way. He won't chase me. At least till I upload to the Web.* Connan called for the housekeeper, Hannah, to set up a conference call for him in his bedroom. Daryn showed up before her.

"Decide to call him earlier? If you tell him anything . . . ."

Connan shook his head. "I decided not to wait till he called me . . . And tell him what? You're already leaving for a bigger opportunity.

What would I say? Daryn got a job with the Mafia; that's why he's leaving me."

"I thought you were past that?" Daryn folded his arms over his chest.

Connan shrugged. "Everyone always leaves me . . . Why would I care if you did?" He turned away. "Must be a real jerk when no one wants to be around you . . . ."

"Connan, that's . . . I'm sorry, kid." Daryn tried to console him. "You could go with me?"

"I'd only be in your way, and if you have to murder someone for Drummond, I'd probably turn you in . . . Just leave . . . Everyone does eventually." Hannah entered the room and started setting up the call.

"I'm not gone yet." Daryn put a hand on Connan's shoulder. "Can we make our last night together a good one? Are you going to try and convince your dad to let you go?"

"Maybe he will let me take the job if I take the initiative to call him first. He should be in his room now." Connan helped Hannah with the rest of the setup. "Daryn, can you stay? It helps my . . . ."

"Courage?" Daryn smiled. "I'll sit in the corner, out of the way. That way he won't think I put you up to this."

"Thanks!" Connan smiled. "You're the best! I still can't believe you're leaving me." Connan sighed. "Guess I'll survive without you though if Dad changes his mind."

Hannah handed him a remote. "All you have to do is hit the call button. I'll be right outside if you need anything." She left the room.

"Thanks, Hannah!" He called after her. He took a deep breath. "Here goes nothing . . . ."

"You can do it." Daryn winked at him.

"Right." Connan pushed the call button and his TV screen came to life. Within a few moments, a much older version of himself appeared on the screen.

"Connan . . . this is a surprise." The man ran a hand through is clean-cut, sandy hair. "I was going to call you a bit later."

"I figured you would . . . I couldn't wait." Connan squared his shoulders. "I'm sorry I lost my temper, Dad."

Todd raised his eyebrows. "You? Apologizing? What happened, I finally knock some sense into you?"

Connan ignored the comment. "Dad, I really want this job. I want to go. I already committed unless you called Sergeant Tibbens. I shouldn't have lost my temper, I know, but I thought you would be happy for me! This is the opportunity of a lifetime! It is the first step to a career in the Marines."

"So . . ." His father's tone hardened. "This is why you are apologizing . . . hoping I'll let you go all the way to the East Coast if you play nicely, is that it?"

Connan took a deep breath. "Dad, I really am sorry. I thought if I called you, it may help. You wouldn't need to hire a new bodyguard since I'll be on base and I would be there till next spring. I'd have holidays off . . . I didn't know you were making plans to go rock climbing and rafting next week. I could ask Sergeant to delay my start date if you like."

"You aren't going to give up on this, are you?"

Connan nodded his head. "I've been waiting on this offer since Sarge mentioned it last fall . . . What do I have to do for you to say yes?"

"For starters, don't beg. It's not very becoming on my son. Second, no more taking the fall for your so-called friends at that tech hangout of yours. I won't bail you out of jail again."

"It was one time, Dad."

Todd raised an eyebrow. "Just one time? You took the fall for Alex's drug stash, you were caught with a fake ID trying to get into a bar with both him and Johnny, you took the fall for Johnny when he . . . ."

"I get the point . . . It's been multiple times . . . Another reason for me to go to North Carolina, I'll have better mentors around me. Sam is going too."

Todd's eyes widened, but he remained calm. "Your battle buddy Sam?"

"Yes."

Todd sighed. "When would you have to leave?"

"Technically, I should've already left . . . so latest would be tomorrow morning . . . ."

"So I wouldn't be able to see you off then . . . ?"

Connan stuffed his hands in his pockets. "Not unless you fly home tonight. Sorry."

"You aren't making this easy on me, son . . ."

"I know."

"Lucky for you, I called your Sergeant yesterday evening. He's very persistent about you joining his team as a platoon leader. He thinks it will be good for you . . ." Todd paused. "You can go, but I expect a call every chance you get."

Connan jerked his hands out of his pockets. "You mean it! I can go?"

"You can go."

Connan grinned. "Thanks Dad! I . . . I won't let you down! I promise!"

Todd shook his head. "Take a burner phone from my office. It will have to do till I can send your phone to you. I'll let Hannah know to let you in. There is an emergency cash envelope in there you can take as well. I take it you want to ride?"

Connan showed his teeth. "As long as that's alright with you? I'll need my bike to get around out there when off duty."

"I would prefer you fly, but it will cost you less to ride the bike than to ship it. Make sure you stay safe."

"I will!" Connan couldn't help the excitement. Daryn was grinning from ear to ear too. "I will send you a copy of the route I'm taking! Sergeant Tibbens will know to call you if I don't make it there by Friday!"

"I'll try to call you in the morning, but I can't promise you I will be able to. Our client will be testifying tomorrow, so it will be a long day."

"I understand. I'll text you when I get to my first stop!"

"You better," Todd replied with a smile. "Take care of yourself, son."

"I will!" Connan watched the screen go blank. *I may not ever hear his voice again. I'm glad we made up.* Connan looked at Daryn. "How'd I do?"

Daryn clapped slowly. "Looks like I'm not the only one packing tonight!"

Connan grinned. "Best get to it if I want to leave after dinner!"

Daryn stood. "I'm going to miss you, kid."

"I'll miss you too . . . Daryn, you're the closest friend I have . . . I still wish you wouldn't work for Drummond. The guy's a complete psycho."

"I know," the tall man sighed. "But you will be busy from now on out. You won't need me. And the money outweighs the cons of the job."

"I need to pack. I really don't need to take a lot. A few changes of clothes and my laptop. Just about everything else is already at the academy! Oh, I should probably go have

Hannah let me into Dad's office! I Should probably take my gaming stuff to the safe. I won't need it at the academy."

"Are you going to place that virus of yours on his computer?"

Connan thought for a moment. "I really don't want to be the one to break the news . . . Maybe over holiday I will take him to the cafe and Mom will show up with one of her boyfriends . . . I don't want to be the one it comes from."

"Probably a good idea. He would know it was you if you put it on his computer."

Connan stretched. "Well, gonna go find Hannah. I'll see you at dinner!" Connan picked up his backpack and headed to the door. Daryn followed him out.

Hannah let Connan into Todd's office which he always locked. Connan decided to encrypt an email and leave it in his dad's personal email. It took him longer than he had expected. *He never opens his personal mail until he's home. He can discover Mom's cheating ways through that and it won't be connected to me.* He grabbed a burner phone and texted his dad to confirm it worked. He then took an envelope from the safe labeled: *Emergency use only.*

He found a credit card and five thousand cash in it. He stuffed it in his bag and put his gaming things in the safe. He did not want to take them or let anyone in the house use them while he was gone. They would only be a distraction and he didn't want to be caught off guard. This is how things got damaged. He returned to his room and packed a few changes of clothes and a small bag of hygiene items. He was ready for his trip. Connan sat down in the dining room with Daryn and Hannah. Hannah had been crying.

"Are you alright, Hannah?" Connan asked.

"I'm losing my two best house occupants . . ." She sniffed. "I'll miss you both."

Connan couldn't help but smile at Daryn. "We must be the most important here."

"To Hannah, we are," Daryn replied. "No one here likes your mom and your dad is gone all the time. We are the only ones who really care about her."

"Very true!" Connan put his hand on Hannah's arm. "I promise to call every chance I get! I'm really going to miss your lasagna! Maybe now you will have time to take a vacation instead of looking after us all the time!"

"I will make sure to give you the occasional call as well." Daryn dipped his head to the gray-headed woman.

"You two . . ." Her lower lip began to tremble. "You always know how to cheer my soul."

3

CONNAN HUGGED HANNAH goodbye and shook Daryn's hand which pulled him into a rough hug. "Stay safe, kid." He let him go and watched as Connan disappeared into the shed. Connan's phone rang.

"Dad? What's up?"

"Sergeant Tibbens said you called late last night and refused the job, why did you beg me to go? Is someone threatening you? Why did you use our distress word *Sam*?"

"I'm not far enough away to tell you . . . All I can say right now is don't get on your plane Friday. I'll explain later, but I need to get out of here before Daryn suspects something is wrong."

"Is Daryn threatening you?"

"I'm sorry, Dad, but you will know soon enough. Keep an eye on the Web."

Connan hung up the phone, placed his helmet on his head, and opened the garage doors. *The sooner I get away the better.* He took hold of his bike and kicked the stand up. Pushing it out of the garage, he could see Daryn still on the porch with Hannah. *Nothing . . . That's either good or bad.* He climbed on his bike and turned the key. He waved one last time to the two on the marble stairs of the mansion before turning toward the front gate.

Twenty minutes later, Connan was parked behind the hotel Debra Hyatt was staying in with her Tuesday boyfriend. *If I remember right, Tuesday rents room 213 . . . Better take the decals off my bike . . . I don't want anyone recognizing it.* He pulled the stickers off and put them in the dumpsters before proceeding to the front of the building. He couldn't help but watch every shadow. No one would suspect him of going to see his mom before leaving. After all, she may wonder why she never sees him at his favorite hangout. *Highly doubt she'll even know I'm gone.*

He went directly to room 213 after confirming Tuesday was there. He banged hard on the door. *Please have clothes on!* A man opened the door a sliver and Connan pushed his way in. His mom lay on the bed with a robe on. He turned away when he saw her. *And no clothes!* She immediately closed the front and crossed her legs.

"Connan!"

He turned back around and pointed at her. "Look, I don't care who you're with, but if you let slip that I was here I will not hesitate to show every boyfriend you have to Dad. I'm here because it's Tuesday and I need a haircut." He turned toward Tuesday. "Get your clippers and give me a Marine's cut. I'm leaving tonight for the academy if anyone comes asking, and I'm sure they will. Keep your mouth shut all together and Dad doesn't have to know about any of this."

Tuesday got his clippers and set to work immediately. Not wanting to be discovered by Debra's dangerous husband, he made sure the haircut was perfect. Connan left them without a goodbye or even a thanks. "I'm warning you.

If anyone comes asking questions of any kind and your lips start moving about the haircut or even seeing me, Dad will kill you both!" Connan left the hotel leaving his bike where it was and went over to The Network.

Liz, the bubbly employee who always wore anime costumes to work, greeted him. "Hi! Nice haircut, Connan. Staying a while?" She smiled sweetly.

"No. Is Johnny in?"

"He's upstairs in VIP. Want a pass?"

"Yes, thank you, and if anyone asks . . . I went to the computer room, not upstairs."

"Okay . . ." Liz looked at him suspiciously, but handed him the pass.

The VIP lounge was meant for anyone over the age of eighteen. Any under the age could only have a fifteen-minute pass. Connan swiped the guest pass and climbed the stairs at the back of the lobby. He found his friend in a corner with his laptop open.

"Johnny," He waved. "Can you spare a minute?"

"Hey! What's up? Haven't seen you here in a while."

"Dad was in town till yesterday . . . I need a favor . . . ."

Johnny gave him a serious look. "You look stressed, man, what's going on?"

Connan pulled out his laptop and played the video for him. "I need a fake ID, a good one."

"What kind of backstory?" Johnny asked.

"Make me seventeen and a troubled foster kid. Kids disappear into the foster system all the time. I can disappear there. Give me a record too . . . some of the stuff I was booked for when I helped you and Alex out of jams; Daryn doesn't know the half of what I've done for you two. Only knows the times I was actually caught. I'll need a bike plate too."

"I'm guessing your gonna post that vid on social media?"

"I'm going to blow it up all over the Internet. Share it as much as you can and make sure Alex does too."

"It will take me a few for a new ID and plate . . . Bring your bike down past the cafe and I'll meet you at my van." Johnny closed his laptop and stood up. "I kept a list of all the scrapes you got us out of so should have your file together by the time the ID prints."

They parted outside and Connan walked to his bike. He put his helmet back on and pushed his bike out to the street. He didn't want to draw attention to himself till he was ready to hit the road. Johnny's van wasn't far.

"Here," Johnny handed him a new bike plate as he got to the side of the van. "I need a picture for your new license."

Connan took his helmet off and climbed into his friend's van. Johnny took a picture and uploaded it to the new ID. "I gave you the name Razor Dallas. You have a sealed juvenile record and have bounced from foster home to foster home since your parents died in a car crash. You are now seventeen as you asked and your new bike plate has already been put into the registry. If you get into trouble I'll put my number as an emergency contact. Need anything else? Cash? A burner phone?"

"I got that already from Dad's office. I owe you one for this." Connan watched his new identity start to print. "I'm gonna get that plate on. Got a screwdriver?"

By the time Connan had placed his new plate on the bike and thrown the old away, his new ID was ready. He put it in his wallet. "Thanks again, Johnny. Like I said, I owe you one."

"Nah," Johnny replied. "We're even now. You took the fall for the stolen plates a few weeks back. Consider this the payback I owe you or at least part of it." Johnny smiled at his friend. "Be careful, CJ."

"I will, thanks." Connan placed his helmet back on his head. "Keep an eye on your feed. I'll be posting the video once I reach The Network that's right off the highway. Make sure your friends share it too. May want to lay low for a while."

Johnny waved as his friend turned his bike on and took off. Connan watched him stroll back toward The Network in his rearview mirrors. *He's one of my only friends. More like a brother than a friend. I'll never forget this!* He watched his speed through town and fifteen minutes later clocked into The Network right off the main highway heading east out of Denver. He plugged his computer in and started his upload. He uploaded to his social media sites with the caption *"Share this!!! Save My Dad!!!"* He pressed enter. A few seconds later, his posts were live. He turned off his laptop and stuffed it back into his backpack. *Now to get out of Denver!*

Connan went as fast as the speed limit allowed down the highway, not daring to stop till his fuel gage had hit a quarter tank. He stopped at the next exit to refuel and grab an energy drink. By morning, he had already crossed half of Missouri. His frequent refueling stops and energy drinks kept him awake for the most part. He received a text in the early morning hours from his dad telling him to be careful and to be smart. He knew at that moment the video had gone viral. *Daryn is definitely going to know now. Hopefully he stays away from Johnny and Alex!*

Connan was becoming tired as he passed through Effingham, Illinois. The energy drinks were no longer keeping him awake. His body was utterly exhausted. Still, he pressed on. *I'll stop once I get through Indianapolis. I can go a few more hours.* A quick refuel and some food helped push away the exhaustion just enough for him to reach the Indiana line. He pulled off at the welcome center and walked around for a few minutes before returning to his bike. It was early afternoon by the time he hit the east side of Indianapolis. He pushed himself even further. *I have to get as much distance as I can!*

Connan made a promise to himself to sleep once he found an exit with a hotel. Even a motel would be fine at this point. A park bench even sounded like the perfect bed. Thirty minutes later he entered the city limits of New Crosley. He blinked slowly.

"No, no, no, no, no!" He lost control of his bike as he tried to miss the giant-sized pothole in front of him. The bike leaned and began to slide sideways. Connan landed on his back hard. He slid with the bike a few feet before freeing his leg. He jumped up as quickly as his tired body allowed and ran after his bike. It had not gone far. He picked it back up and pushed the kick stand down with his foot.

"Looks like it only damaged the body . . ." Connan took his helmet off and assessed his own movement. *My ankle is a bit sore but I don't think I was hurt. My backpack took the brunt of the fall.* He sat down on the side of the road. *I knew I shouldn't have pushed myself so hard. But I needed to create a lot of space between me and Daryn.* He leaned forward, resting his elbows on his knees, and ran his hands through his short hair.

He was about to fall asleep right there on the side of the road when a siren caught his attention. He looked up. *Someone must have seen me go down and called 911.* He watched as the squad car's siren went silent and the officer parked at an angle to protect both himself and Connan. A tall, balding man stepped out of the car.

"Are you okay?" The cop approached with caution, his hand on his firearm.

"Yes, sir," Connan replied. "I about fell asleep and didn't see the pothole back there. Over corrected and laid my bike down. I'll be alright."

Shocked at how young the rider looked, the officer relaxed. "Why don't we have a medic check you over anyway. You look exhausted. I will also need to have a look at your license." The officer got on his radio and instructed dispatch to keep the medic coming. "You could have internal injuries you don't know about yet."

"Alright, but I wasn't going that fast so I doubt I have any internal issues." Connan thought it best not to argue with a cop. He knew arguing with one usually ended up with him in handcuffs. *The only issue I have right now is no sleep and not enough space between me and Daryn.* He fished out his wallet and took out his fake license. *Johnny's merch is good. Hopefully the cop doesn't figure out its fake.*

4

OTHER THAN BEING utterly exhausted, Connan felt fine. After the medic gave him a clean bill of health, He went back and picked up his helmet. The officer, whose name tag read "*Cap. Rigby,*" stopped him.

"You shouldn't be riding with how tired you look." His brown eyes scanned over Connan like an X-ray machine.

"Home is a two-day ride west, and I got about two more days to go before I reach the East Coast. I'll rent a room down the road or something."

"Your license tells me you won't be able to rent a room... You have to be at least eighteen in this state to rent." The officer placed his thumbs in his belt. "Why not follow me down to the station. I'm almost done for the evening. You can sleep in my office, and I'll take you to get something to eat once I've finished my reports."

"Thanks for the offer, but I really need to stay on the road as much as possible." Connan went to place his helmet back on.

Captain Rigby persisted. "Look, kid, I'm not going to let you hit the highway again until I know you are rested enough to take on another two days on that thing. I'm not going to let you kill yourself." He pointed at Connan's bike. "You know, I don't think you should ride at all." Before Connan could even protest, Captain Rigby was on his radio calling for a bike tow. "If I have to arrest you, I will. You aren't leaving till you get some rest and the safest place to do that around here is at the station. Now will you come willingly or do I have to cuff you?"

"You're not giving me another option." Connan's knuckles turned white as he gripped his helmet. *Why do cops always have to intervene!* "I'd rather not be arrested."

The captain smiled and gestured to his squad car. "Shall we, then? We will wait till the tow arrives for your bike before we leave."

Connan placed his helmet in the front seat along with his backpack but was instructed to sit in the back. "Not that I don't trust you, kid, but this way you can't bail on me."

Connan decided not to say anything. He was too angry at the man to not get arrested if he did. He couldn't help it. He thought about all the ways he could possibly get out of this situation, but everything he thought of ended with him in handcuffs and being discovered. *I should've taken Dad's credit cards out of my wallet before I left home . . . If he snoops, I'm as good as dead . . . I'll just tell him I stole it . . . That would go over well . . .* Connan closed his eyes, he really didn't want to blow up at the cop especially when he didn't get along with any he met. Within a few seconds he was out. He couldn't stay awake.

"What part of Colorado you from, Mr. Dallas?" Captain Rigby looked in his rearview mirror. "And that's why I kept you here . . ." He shook his head. He picked up his work phone and speed dialed dispatch. "Hey, Barb, can you place me out of service for the rest of my shift? I picked up the kid who wrecked his bike. He's too young for a hotel room and I'm not letting him kill himself by driving off . . . Not a minute passed after he slid into the car and he was out . . . I'm bringing him back to the station. He can rest in my office while I finish out my shift reports . . . I also want to look into him a bit more. I can't think of any logical reason a seventeen-year-old would be riding halfway across the nation unsupervised unless he's running from something or another . . . Thanks, Barb, talk to you later."

Connan didn't wake up till Captain Rigby opened the back door for him at the station. "I'm glad I could convince you to stay."

"I didn't have a choice in the matter." Connan scowled.

"Oh, now the attitude comes out," Rigby laughed. "You need more sleep, kid, otherwise I may have to lock you up for smarting off . . . Come on." Rigby handed him his pack, but kept the helmet. "We'll keep this in the office till I let you go."

Connan bit back another rude comment. *Holding cells are not a comfortable place to be. Might as well be under arrest the way he's acting though . . .* Connan could only think back on the time his friend Alex was carrying illegal drugs in the mall. Two officers had pulled up as they had exited. Connan had pocketed the drugs so his friend wouldn't go to jail and tried to beat the cops to the restroom and destroy the evidence. It hadn't worked. Daryn stopped by the station to tell him his dad wasn't going to let him bail him out because of the reason being drugs. Two days later Todd himself bailed him out and his record was wiped clean. He had been grounded for two months for that stunt.

He followed Captain Rigby to an office on the second floor. He slouched in a corner of the sofa that graced the front wall of the space. *Should probably make sure I didn't break my laptop. The hard drive is the only thing that has the original video other than Alex's phone.* He pulled the computer out. "Great . . ." He mumbled. The screen had spiderwebbed and the lid was cracked. He placed it back in his backpack. And grabbed his wallet. *I don't want him finding out who I am and he will if he snoops!*

"We'll be here a few hours, so why not get some rest. I gotta make a quick call to my wife."

Captain Rigby left Connan in his office and went out in the hall. He dialed a number. "Hey, hun . . . How was the game? . . . Derek did what? . . . I bet his coach was really proud of him for that! . . . She wants to go where? . . . May as well, but can you set a plate out anyway? . . . I am bringing a guest for dinner . . . No, he's just a kid . . . I haven't looked into him yet, but he needs a good meal and some proper sleep before I let him move on . . . Thanks, honey, I'll see you in a few hours." He hung up and went back in his office. He found Connan already asleep again.

"Let's see what we can find on you," He whispered. He started typing on his keyboard. *Razor Dallas . . . No parents since 2004 . . . Date of birth . . . Now, that's interesting, frequent runner . . .* He scrolled down farther. *No wonder he shut up when I mentioned lock up, he's been there before . . . Marijuana possession and consumption.* He looked over his desktop at Connan. *I want to check his ID again, and his bag . . . If he's been in for drugs, he's definitely not taking any under my roof.* He silently crept around his desk and searched through the backpack. Connan was fast asleep again and oblivious to the world around him.

Captain Rigby searched through the backpack. When he couldn't find the wallet, he looked over Connan. *What are you hiding . . . ?* He spotted it in Connan's hand. He carefully slid the wallet out and took it back to his desk. *Why would you try and hide this from me?* He opened it and spread the contents on his desk. *Credit cards under Todd Hyatt? Why would he have . . . And a card for Connan Hyatt . . . Why do I know those names?* He opened his Web search engine and typed in *Todd Hyatt*. A video tube broadcast popped up in his search along with several videos labeled *"Murder Plot Thwarted by 16-Year-Old."* He turned his volume down and clicked on one of the news pages.

"Yesterday evening, around 8 p.m., this video went viral on social media." The woman was cut out and the video that Connan had taken popped up and was played. "As, you have just seen, the video depicts a murder plot against a witness protection agent in the private sector by the name of Todd Hyatt. The video was taken and uploaded by Agent Hyatt's only child, Connan Hyatt. Authorities have yet to locate him. His mother, Debra Hyatt, and their housekeeper both say he was headed for North Carolina to a military school where he claimed to have gotten a job for the summer. Authorities contacted the school and reported that Connan had declined the job and the trail has gone cold for the investigators. They will be filing a missing person report. His two friends, who did not want to be named, told authorities that he has gone into hiding, where, they did not know. He is rumored to be making his way to his father. Authorities have not been able to track down the men in the video clip at this point. Further investigations will be made by the detectives at DPD. This is Cecil Moriarti reporting live, EDC News."

Captain Rigby stared at the screen. *Lord, I don't know if you did this, but you brought him to the right place at the right time . . . He needs us . . . Thank you, Jesus, for guiding him to us and out of harm's way.* Captain Rigby brought Connan's file back up and made some adjustments. *I'm guessing his friends made this . . . definitely not a professional job, but that should do the trick. The ID is almost spot on. Whoever he went through knows how to make a good fake . . . the file I would say was a first attempt. I need to contact the county . . . and Grace.*

5

AFTER A LENGTHY phone call to the county and a briefing with his chief, Captain Rigby dialed his wife's number again. "Hey, I still have to finish reports, but I wanted to run something by you . . . Yes . . . The kid I'm bringing for supper . . . He's in a lot of trouble . . . No, not that kind of trouble, his life could be in serious danger . . . I'll explain when we get there, but I want to blend him into our family . . . just for a little while . . . He needs a cover and, with the fake file I found, I think we can give him that . . . His file says he's a foster from Colorado Springs . . . I made the call to the county to have him transferred to our foster care since the family he was with wanted him gone . . . No, the number for the foster family turned out to be a friend of his, I think. Probably the same one that made the fake ID and profile. What do you think . . . ? That was my thought exactly . . . Alright, I'll see you later."

Not five minutes after hanging up with his wife the county called again. "Hello? . . . yes, this is Captain Rigby . . . So the transfer is a go? Great! . . . No need, he's already in my custody . . . Apparently he had plans to run away and made it this far . . . I will take care of it, thank you . . . same to you, bye." *Once the fax comes through I can sign and he will have a legal cover. He's not going to be happy about it. I'll have to ask him about the drugs though.* Rigby picked up the helmet and took it to two of his officers.

"You know the bike I had towed in? Take it to the impound lot and put this in the evidence locker. Don't log either, if the guys down there have a problem with that, have them call me or the chief."

The two men nodded with a "Yes, sir" and left the room. Two hours later, Rigby had finished all his reports. *He's still sleeping . . .*

He would probably sleep well into tomorrow if I let him. He wadded up a piece of paper and threw it at Connan. He didn't stir, so Rigby repeated his paper tossing a few more times. He sighed, got up, and walked over to the sofa. He nudged Connan's left shoulder and jumped back. *Probably shouldn't startle him too much.* He had to repeat this a few times before Connan opened his eyes.

"Rise and shine, sleeping beauty." Rigby returned to his desk. He placed Connan's cards back in his wallet and threw it to him as he sat up. "It's a good thing, I found you and not the people you're running from."

Connan, alarmed, whipped his head around toward the door then down at the wallet in his hand. His anger started to rise, but he held his tongue. *Please, don't put me in lock up to try and protect me! I can do this on my own!*

"I have impounded your bike without registering it and did the same with your helmet in the evidence locker. You will be staying with me for a while."

"You impounded my bike!" Connan couldn't keep the enraged explosion from happening. "I can't stay here! I have to keep moving or he will find me! You can't just do that!"

"I can and I did." Rigby kept his voice calm. "Your fake ID is registered as a foster teen and I just happen to be a foster parent of four boys. You will take cover with us whether you like it or not. It's already legally binding for Razor Dallas. I'm not going to let an endangered sixteen-year-old loose knowing I can help keep you safe."

"I don't need your help." Connan glared at the man, but he lowered his tone, not wanting to draw attention to the office.

"Whether you want it or not, you have it. I have the final say in this if you don't want to go into lockup like a common criminal. Now, I need to know if what your file says is true . . . Have you been in possession of marijuana?"

Connan didn't say anything.

John eyed him. "I take it then, you have."

"It was one time, okay!" Connan leaned forward, resting his elbows on his knees. "Dad and I had a fight over the phone and I was with Alex. I got into his stash . . . Ended up being so sick, I crashed with mom and her Thursday doctor appointment because I knew my bodyguard would tell on me. I never did it again. Once was enough!"

Captain Rigby thought for a minute as if wondering if he should believe him or not. "And the joyriding?"

Connan rolled his eyes. "I've lost count of how many times we did that . . . There were only two instances where the cops chased us and we got away . . . Why am I even telling you this? That info is enough to put me away!"

"Do you want to go to jail?"

"No."

"Then, this confession of yours wasn't heard by me. Of course, if you argue, I will make sure it goes in front of a judge." Rigby stood and grabbed a coat on top of his filing cabinet. "Get your pack and let's go. Dinner is at seven and we aren't going to be late."

Connan didn't want to argue with a second threat of lockup in play. *He may just do it if I keep fighting him on this. Dad would've already kicked me around and forced me. This guy's threats, I'm sure, shouldn't be taken lightly . . . Stupid good doers, always getting in the way!* He kept glaring at Rigby, but kept his mouth shut. He did not want to end up in the county jail.

This time, Connan was allowed to sit in the front of the squad car. He didn't look at the officer. *This is stupid! He can't hold me! I should be on my way to the base! Maybe I can sneak off tonight ... If he doesn't have a security system.*

Connan soon found out what kind of security the family of fosters had. As they pulled in the drive, a donkey started braying. A black German Shepherd ran from behind the house along with two boys. Connan thought they looked a lot alike. Rigby shut the car off and turned to Connan.

"I know you don't like this little arrangement, but disrespect my wife and you will have bigger problems, got that."

"Yea, I got it ..." Connan snapped. "I'll play nice." He stared out the window, not daring to look at the man. *He's nothing like Dad. I don't know how he will respond so probably shouldn't be a pain.* "Daryn will still find me here ... You're just putting your family in danger."

"I've been at my job probably longer than you've been alive. You let me worry about Daryn ... and don't step out till I get a hold of Bailey." Rigby opened his door and called the dog.

Is he speaking German? There goes the sneaking out idea ... Can't go anywhere without my bike and, if I go to the station, they will just hold me till Cap here comes to get me. Rigby motioned that it was safe to step out. The dog sniffed the air and began to growl. Connan kept his eyes low. *Don't make eye contact like the K-9 unit taught.* He stopped when he got close enough to make the dog start barking. He knelt and kept his eyes on the ground. The dog sniffed at him and began to settle down. Connan stood back up.

"What was that about?" Rigby raised an eyebrow. "He hates strangers and you let him get close enough to kill you if he wanted."

Connan shrugged. "I showed him I wasn't going to challenge him . . . that's all."

"So he's your best friend now?"

"No," Connan avoided his gaze. "I'm just not a threat to him anymore."

Rigby let go of the dog's collar and watched him trot off around the house. "Don't think he won't chase if you try to sneak out."

"I'm not that stupid, he wouldn't recognize me in the dark and would definitely give chase. Learned that lesson at school . . . Not to mention the donkey on duty." Connan looked around at all the animals. The Rigbys not only had a donkey and a dog. They also had chickens, ducks, a couple cats, and a few goats. He looked at the boy who hadn't moved since they pulled up to the house.

"Lose the attitude," Rigby warned. "This is Derek. He and his brothers have been with us for two years. Troy, the youngest, came to us six months ago . . . Come on."

Connan followed the captain into the house. The hall was only wide enough for one person to enter at a time. He waited while Rigby took his shoes off. He followed his actions and took his own boots off. *Don't want to disrespect his wife by getting the floor dirty. Hannah would kill me if I dirtied her floors.* Rigby led the way into a large open kitchen that had an island in the middle. A small boy sat on a stool on one side of it eating apple slices.

"Daddy!" He scrambled down from the stool and ran toward Rigby with his arms stretched out.

Not missing a beat, Captain Rigby picked the toddler up and threw him in the air. "Troy! Have you been good today?" The little boy nodded and hugged him around the neck. Rigby went farther in. "Where's mommy?" Troy pointed at a door on the opposite wall.

Rigby crossed the room and opened the door. A boy, who looked identical to Derek, ran up the stairs on the other side. His brown hair matched his eyes. "She's coming! James superglued his hands to a controller."

"He what?!" Rigby charged down the stairs after putting Troy down. The boy that had come up the stairs dipped his head to Connan.

"Hi, I'm Dean."

"Razor." Connan didn't dare use his real name.

"Cool name!" Dean smiled. "You'll fit right in around here!"

Connan just huffed in reply. He looked around the room still too angry to not be careful with his words. The dining room was open to the kitchen and the chairs looked worn. Connan could tell they actually ate as a family. It was worn and looked as if it needed a new coat of stain and polish. Dean motioned for him to follow him saying, "Let me show you around!" The living room sat just beyond the dining room with a large sectional cutting the two spaces in half. *Great, bunch of Bible-thumpers,* Connan thought as he noticed a corner table with a well-worn book on it. The golden letters no longer shined from the years of use. On the left was another door that Dean said was the downstairs bathroom.

A hall led to the master bedroom, a locked office, the back door, and a guest room.

"This is where you're staying! Kind of jealous, I've always wanted this room, but I share with my twin." Dean took him upstairs to the three bedrooms and bathroom up there. The largest bedroom was his sister's room and the other two rooms were split between the twins, James and Troy. "Tracy will spend all morning in the bathroom so expect a line downstairs!" Dean rolled his eyes as if to say "Girls . . . ."

They descended the stairs and Connan dumped his backpack on the bed that was now his. He took his laptop back out and a small tool kit he carried. He checked it over again. *Screen could be replaced but with the lid cracked, it probably took more damage. I'll have to take it apart and see if I can fix it. If I can't salvage it, I'll just take the hard drive out and buy a new computer.*

A knock on the door frame of the room made him jump. Connan turned to see Captain Rigby standing there. "I would like you to come meet my wife." Connan nodded and followed him back to the living room. A middle-aged woman with a laundry basket on her hip stood near the kitchen stove. She stirred the contents of a pot then placed the lid back on. She was a shorter woman with dark red hair that curled up at the nape of her neck. She was thin but looked strong. She smiled at him.

"I'm Grace, we're glad to have you with us, Razor!" Her soft voice crooned a level of trust she held for the people around her.

"Yea, thanks . . ." With a look from the Captain, Connan added, "Nice to meet you."

Grace had gone on with her duties as if she had not seen the interaction or heard the rest of the sentence. Troy was now trying to wrap himself around her leg and her attention had shifted. Captain Rigby got as close to Connan's ear as he could.

"Don't get smart with her just because you don't want to be here. She does a lot for this family, and she will be respected. Did they not teach you manners at school?" His authoritative voice made Connan's skin crawl.

It was uncomfortable how much this man was acting like a father toward him. *Just not as quick to get angry and fight like Dad,* he had thought. He nodded his understanding. "I'm not exactly one of their best students." He held up his laptop. "I need to work on this. Got a space?"

Captain Rigby nodded. "I can see that. You can work on it at the island. There's more light there." Rigby retired to a corner recliner and picked up his Bible. He was in clear view of the kitchen.

He just wants to keep an eye on me... Connan took his laptop and tool kit to the kitchen. As he started to take the laptop's backing off, the twins appeared at his side.

"Mind if we watch?" Connan thought it was Dean who spoke. Derek hadn't said a word to him. This was the only difference Connan could see other than Dean being a bit bulkier in build than his twin.

"Knock yourself out, just watch the glass." Connan kept taking the laptop apart, examining every piece he took out. He sighed, shaking his head as he looked at the insides of his computer.

"Is it fixable?" Dean asked.

"No, the motherboard is wrecked . . . The hard drive should still work but the rest has to be junked." Connan scanned the room for a trash can. "Do you have a bag I could put this in before tossing it? I don't want sharp corners cutting the trash bag open."

"Yea!" Dean opened a drawer near the bottom of the island and drew out a bag. "This work?"

"Yea, that should work." Connan finished disassembling the computer and put its pieces in the bag Dean had grabbed for him. He saved the hard drive. Everything else was trashed. Connan placed his tools back in their case and stood up. "Captain?"

Rigby looked up at him, his Bible open in his hands. "What is it?"

"You got a safe place for this? It holds a video that needs to be protected."

Rigby stood and held out his hand for the hard drive. "I'll lock it in the safe."

"Thanks." Connan handed over the hard drive and went on cleaning up his mess.

He jumped when Grace asked, "Did the glass break on the counter?"

"There could be particles left behind." He went to rub the counter down with his hand, but Grace stopped him. She took a cloth out of a drawer near the sink and wet it. "Use this, otherwise you will have glass embedded in your hand."

Connan thanked her and wiped the counter down. Dean started asking him a lot of questions while Derek just stared at him.

"Do you play video games? Do you like Rise of the Zombies? Want to play a few rounds? Have you ever heard of . . . ?"

"Don't you have chores to do?" Rigby cut in as he walked back down the hall toward them. "Animals get fed before you do, and dinner is about done . . . I can smell it." Rigby sat back down in his chair.

Dean hung his head and motioned for his twin to follow. They disappeared out of the front door moments later. Connan took his tool kit back to his room then made himself comfortable on the sectional in front of Rigby. "Is there something wrong with the other twin?"

6

IT WAS EXPLAINED to Connan that Derek was diagnosed with autism and that he didn't speak. They had never heard his voice and didn't think they ever would. "Dean says he hasn't talked since their parents died in a fire four years back." Captain Rigby continued. "He's quite the character if you watch him from a distance. James could potentially have the same gene, but we think he has more of Dean's mannerisms than Derek's. Our youngest, Troy, came to us from a woman who overdosed. She was on drugs when she had him and he was born addicted himself. No one wanted a toddler that needed so much care."

"I bet Derek could put a computer together." Connan leaned back and stared at the popcorn ceiling. "He looks the type. He needs something to do with his hands other than video games and goats."

"What do you mean?" Rigby sat up, marked his page with the Bible's ribbon then put it down.

"Well," Connan started. "He doesn't register emotions like a normal kid. He can't connect with people very well. He communicates differently without words or sign language. No one can see it because it's not normal. Give him a computer or some kind of tools where he can put things together, and he will speak in volumes."

"You have experience with autistic kids?"

"Not his age, but two of the employees at The Network have autism. One is just like Derek and doesn't speak. He draws comics and has been rated the number one hometown graphic novelist. He communicates through his art."

"We haven't been able to find anything to bring Derek out of the shadows yet. Dean can't even give us an idea."

"Get him a computer. If you've tried everything else, then maybe he needs to see something new." Connan closed his eyes. "Cameron is a great guy once you learn how to communicate with him." *Dad would've never listened like he just did.* Connan started to feel uncomfortable.

"I'll keep that in mind." The captain stood as his wife entered the room.

"Dinner is ready, would you mind helping set the table while the boys finish their chores?" Grace continued her path to the kitchen. "I'll get everything out if you boys would put it on the table!"

Rigby motioned for Connan to get up. They placed the dinner plates, cups, and silverware for Grace. She threw them hot pads to place the pans on. Their dinner would consist of corn and potatoes, meat loaf, and a simple salad.

"Normally Tracy would help me, but she's at her friends tonight so thank you for the help!" She brought one of the hot pans to the table.

John looked over at Connan. "Tracy is off limits . . . I know how you teenagers think and you will not be allowed to date our daughter, so get it out of your head, now."

"Why would I even want to date someone I haven't even met? Besides, Dean says she's a bathroom hog, and that doesn't turn any guy on unless they are allowed in there with her." Connan tried to hide a laugh as the captain's face went a pale shade of red.

"You best clear your mind of that nonsense before she gets home tomorrow . . . She is very beautiful, like her mother."

"Now you're making me blush!" Grace had went red in the face too.

Wish my parents were like this . . . These two love each other . . . Connan stared, imagining his mom and dad acting like this. He imagined his mom being loyal and his dad complimenting her and imagined his own embarrassment toward their actions.

"Earth to Razor . . ." Captain Rigby waved a hand in front of his face. "Go wash up before we eat."

Connan slowly rose to his feet. "Can I just eat in my room?" After a "No" from Rigby, Connan left the kitchen for the bathroom.

The two smaller boys met him there to wash their hands too.

Captain Rigby hugged his wife and whispered, "I don't think he knows how to act in a family . . . By the sound of it, he's an only child with no parental guidance . . . He might as well be an orphan at this point . . . He must've caused a lot of trouble at that school of his."

"He will get used to us," Grace whispered back. "I don't think he's ever seen love either . . . I saw him fade out just a minute ago . . . He's never seen our kind of love."

"Maybe we are meant to help him in more ways than one." Rigby kissed his wife.

"Yuck!" James bounded into the room, followed by Troy and Connan. "Get a room!" He took a seat at the table. Dean and Derek ran in the front door, took their shoes off, and headed for the bathroom.

Connan kept his distance till everyone else had chosen a seat. He sat down where the last remaining plate had been set. He was thankful it was the farthest spot from the captain.

"Let's bless the food." Captain Rigby bowed his head along with the others. Connan watched. Even Troy had his eyes squeezed tightly shut.

They do everything together ... I've never seen a family so connected, and they aren't even all blood. Bitterness rose in his stomach as a chill ran down his spine. *Why would this god of theirs, if he is good, keep me from a real family?* His mom acted as if he didn't exist and his dad was constantly traveling, always fighting him. The only two in the home that cared about him was now hundreds of miles away and one of them wanted nothing more than to kill him now. *Maybe I should've stayed home and kept my mouth shut.* He pretended to have his head bowed and eyes closed when Rigby said "Amen."

Connan picked at his food. He didn't feel all that hungry. Part of him wanted to run and the other part wanted a better taste of this family life. He stared at his plate. *I feel so out of place ... Why did he have to take my bike?! I can't take ....*

"Hey!" Connan looked up at the head of the table. Captain Rigby was staring him down. "What's wrong?"

Connan hadn't realized how tightly he was holding his fork. His knuckles had turned white. He put the fork down. "Nothing, just tired."

"Outside, now." Captain Rigby got up. Grace shot him a "be gentle" look. Connan rolled his eyes. The whole eating together as a family was a bit much for him to take. It unnerved him. He stood up suddenly in his anger and followed Rigby outside.

"What's the problem, Connan?" Rigby didn't hesitate to make the first move. "Talk to me."

Connan shrugged his shoulders. "I'm just tired." He avoided Rigby's dark, piercing gaze, too angry to look him in the eyes.

"If you were just tired you wouldn't be white knuckled or even tense! In fact the opposite would apply if you were. Talk to me." John's voice was even and controlled.

"Why? I don't know you! No one ever listens anyway! What do you want from me?" Connan said, still not wanting to look at the captain.

"I want you to talk to me." Rigby folded his arms across his broad chest. "I can't help you if you stand here like an angry brick wall."

"I never asked for your help!" Connan mirrored Rigby's stance and finally looked up at him. "I never wanted to be here! I won't just blend in! I've never had siblings let alone a mom that sees me and a dad that actually sticks around! The only one who's ever wanted to listen was Daryn! My best friend; and now he probably wants me dead! I've got nothing to lose if I stay or leave! He's going to find me if I stay! This is just so messed up! I should've stayed home and kept my mouth shut, then this wouldn't have happened! Should've just stayed and let him kill me! I'm better off dead at this poi . . . ."

His words were cut off as Captain Rigby backhanded him across the mouth, making his head jerk to the side. "Stop! Better off dead? Are you kidding me? If you really thought that then you would've let your friend kill you right then and there! Your argument has no basis for you to think like that! You may have nothing to lose, but you have everything in the world to gain!" Rigby paused. "I figured this would be hard on you, but . . . I thought you'd be able to handle it better!"

7

CONNAN WAS STUNNED. He stood there with one hand over his mouth. The slap had stung, but the words stung even deeper. As soon as Rigby had finished, he had jerked the door open and went back inside. Connan slowly sat down on the front porch stairs. He put his face in his hands. Tears threatened to flow, and he started to tremble. *Why does he even care? He doesn't know me! This sucks!*

Rigby stormed into the kitchen and started pacing back and forth.

"John?" Grace got up from the table and went to comfort him. "What happened? Where is . . . ."

"I slapped him, Grace. I haven't lost my temper like that since Jesus got a hold of me . . . ."

Grace wrapped him in a hug. "You've never had a troubled teenager in your house either. This is new for him, and us."

"He was talking about just letting this Daryn guy kill him . . . Said he'd be better off dead . . . That's when I lost it . . ." Rigby buried his face in his wife's shoulder.

Grace looked at the silent table and all four boys turned back to their plates. "He's confused and hurt and probably feels so alone right now. He doesn't know what a family looks like. It's foreign to him. John, he needs guidance, and you can't help him if you're in here pacing like this. He just lost everything."

Rigby sighed. "You're right . . . I may have overreacted, but he still needs my help. I shouldn't be in here beating myself up and worrying you." He kissed his wife on the forehead. "Thank you."

Grace smiled. "Just try to take it easy on him this time. God will give you the words to say."

Rigby headed for the door again. As he opened it, he caught Connan wiping his eyes. He sat down beside him on the steps. They sat like this for some time. Both quiet and unmoving.

"Look," Rigby said, breaking the silence. "I overstepped...."

"No," Connan cut him off. "I did... I shouldn't have yelled at you." Connan sighed. "That's the first time I've been beat to the punch... Kind of shocked me."

"You and your dad fight a lot?"

Connan lifted his shirt and showed the now black-and-blue bruise on his ribs. "Constantly, I always throw the first punch, though. He never listens so I get mad, then he gets mad; turns into an all-out brawl."

"I shouldn't have hit you, and I am sorry. I don't take kids wanting to kill themselves very lightly."

"It was stupid, heat of the moment... I just ... I've got nothing left."

"There once was a man..." Rigby scratched his head, "who had one hundred sheep. One wondered off and he left the ninety-nine to find the one. When he found it, he put it on his shoulders and came back saying, 'I have found my lost sheep! Celebrate with me!' He went after what most would see as not worth the trouble. But it was everything to him. Never give up, Connan, you're worth more than you will ever know."

"Maybe, but I sure don't feel like it now." Connan leaned forward, resting his elbows on his knees. "No one's ever just tried talking to me before . . . It's always, 'We'll talk later' or 'What do you want?' or 'Now's not the time' or it's a knockdown, drag out fight . . . stuff like that. The only one who ever listened to what I had to say was Daryn. He . . . To him I was more his son than I am Dad's . . . Never heard that story before either."

"It's a parable from the Bible." John paused. "That's the second time you've said that about Daryn. Do you think he would actually kill you?" Rigby looked straight at him.

"I really don't know. He never cared about the pay before now, at least he never let on about it. He wanted me to go with him . . . I may fight with my dad, but I don't hate him. I'd never want him dead."

"Would he send his friends after you?"

"No," Connan looked up at the captain. "He knows I could take them. He wouldn't even let his guys take on Dad. Dad is a far better fighter than I am, but Daryn knows his friends couldn't take me either. I may not have the best attitude at my school, but I hold the fitness and combat record." Connan shook his head. "I can't beat him or Dad."

"So he will have to come after you himself or leave you alone." Rigby sighed. "I'm sorry Connan."

Connan shrugged his shoulders. "It's what it is . . . I guess I never really knew Daryn . . . I never thought he'd be capable of this line of work. He always seemed so . . . anyway." Connan sighed. "Can we go eat now?"

Rigby stood. "As long as you're done trying to kill the plate."

Connan stifled a laugh. "I make no promises. Just for the record this doesn't make us friends."

"Never said it would. You break the plate though Grace is liable to kill you herself . . . Come on." Rigby opened the door and they returned to the dining room.

Connan leaned back in his chair, his plate empty. Grace took his plate and the rest of the boys' plates to the sink. He placed his hands behind his head. Grace smiled at him.

"I'm guessing you enjoyed that?"

"Yeah," he replied. "It was good, thanks."

"You're very welcome!" Grace cleared the table as the boys hit the bath. Connan went to his room and decided to lay down. He dug the burner phone out of his pack. He dialed his dad's number but stopped before pressing the call button. *I probably shouldn't call him. I'll send him a quick text so he doesn't worry*. He pressed the buttons forming the words: *"I'm safe, under cover."* He turned the phone off and stuffed it back in his bag. He closed his eyes. *Maybe I'm better off here than on the road. This cop seems alright. May not like him, but I have more respect for him now than I did. Wonder what that story was really about....*

A couple of hours later, Captain Rigby appeared in the doorway. "Shower's ... And you thought you'd be better off on the road ..." He shook his head.

Connan lay sideways on the bed with his feet hanging off one side and his left arm hung off the end. John quietly closed the door.

Connan slept through the rest of the evening and into the early morning hours. He woke up as sunlight lit up his bedroom. He sat up and stretched. He looked at the closed door. *What a night! Don't think I've slept that well since I snuck out at the academy and got night duty. Had to stay up till the next night.* Connan grabbed the first set of clothes from his pack and his hygiene bag.

Grace was already up and starting breakfast when he opened his door. She told him where he could find the towels and to make sure he got his dirty clothes to her. "We'll have to take you to the mall for more clothes," Grace had said. Connan didn't take long. He put fresh bottoms on and had started brushing his teeth when a knock on the door interrupted him.

James stood dancing at the door. "Please! I need to go and Dean's hogging the bathroom!"

Connan jumped out and let the six-year-old go while he finished brushing his teeth outside the door.

Grace laughed from the kitchen. "Welcome to brotherhood."

Connan tried to smile back but it was a bit hard with a toothbrush and toothpaste in his mouth. He stood outside the door shirtless as

James did his business. The front door opened and Connan heard a girl's voice say goodbye to someone.

"Hey, Mom! Is Dad up yet?" A petite redhead threw her backpack onto the island. Connan choked on the toothpaste in his mouth. James opened the door and Connan ducked in and spit out the contents in his mouth. He finished as quickly as he could.

Not another one! Connan wiped his mouth as Troy was now in the bathroom trying to push him out. "I potty! I potty!" the toddler repeated.

Connan grabbed his dirty clothes and clean shirt and stepped out. The door slammed behind him. Grace and her daughter turned toward him. "It wasn't me!" Connan couldn't say much else. He stood in the living room, still shirtless, with the only two women in the house staring at him.

Grace made her way around the table and took his dirty clothes out of his hands so he could put his shirt on. She looked at the bruise on his ribs with concern. "That looks pretty painful."

"It's nothing, really. I've had worse." Connan tried to hide his embarrassment of being caught without a shirt in front of two women. He had caught the younger version of Grace staring at his chest and abs. He quickly pulled his shirt over his head.

"Do they always do that?" Connan asked as Troy opened the door again. He had left his pants and diaper on the bathroom floor. And began to climb the stairs again.

"You'll get used to it," Grace said with a deep breath. "Mornings are crazy around here, so if you want to beat the rush, you may want to get up a bit earlier."

"I'll remember that. Thanks." Connan glanced up at the redhead who was still staring at him. Grace caught on and turned to her daughter.

"Tracy, come meet the latest edition to our family."

Tracy stepped around the table, blinking rapidly. "Nice to meet you . . . ."

"Hey," Connan replied. He adjusted his shirt. *Don't worry, Cap, she's pretty but she's not my type.* Connan let his thoughts roam before the noise behind him brought him into focus again.

"If it isn't the bathroom hog!" Dean stuck his tongue out at Tracy as he hit the bottom of the stairs.

"Oh and you're one to talk?" Tracy had her hands on her hips. "You would spend all morning in the bathroom too!"

"Not as long as you!" Came the reply.

"Not today!" Grace held her hands up as if playing referee. "None of this nonsense. Dean, chores. Tracy, get your things out of the kitchen please."

Both obeyed at once. Grace opened the door to the basement and disappeared. Connan put his hygiene bag back in his room and found a pair of socks in the bottom of his bag. He sat down and began putting them on. Captain Rigby stopped as he passed Connan's open door.

"Up already?" Rigby asked. "I figured you would still be sleeping!"

Connan gave him a half smile and stood up. "Can't really sleep when the room lights up this bright."

"Did you get to meet Tracy?"

"Yeah, and don't worry, Cap. She's definitely not my type." Connan smiled. "I'm more into blonds. She doesn't seem to get along very well with Dean . . . ."

"They fight like cats and dogs." Rigby laughed. "True brother and sister style if you ask me . . . She will probably ask if you will run with her. She's trying to make the track team come fall semester."

"Not that I can't run, but I hate running. They make us do two miles every morning before classes all school year. I always finish first because I'd rather it be over then prolong it like some of the students." Connan stood. "Only thing that would persuade me to run is that dog . . . or Daryn."

"He's not going to find you." Rigby gave him a stern look. "He is expecting you on the East Coast tomorrow morning."

Connan shrugged. "Maybe he is maybe he isn't. Maybe he expects me to stay in one place because he knows that I know he knows me, so he looks for me as if he's me and that's going to . . . ."

"Stop." Rigby warned. "I know you're scared but fretting about what might happen isn't going to help anyone." He paused to let his words sink in. "Why don't you help me repair the goat pin after breakfast? It will get your mind off of things. We'll be on babysitting duty as well. Grace is going grocery shopping.

"Joy . . . Do I have a choice?" Connan replied.

"Not really, no." Rigby answered. "I'm not going to let you sit around and sulk all day."

8

GRACE SAID GOODBYE after breakfast, taking Troy with her. Tracy was left on kitchen clean up while the rest of them headed outside. There were three holes in the fence that needed fixing. Captain Rigby and Connan were in charge of fixing the holes and the younger boys were to keep the goats from getting out while they worked.

Connan found the work satisfying. He had never helped repair anything or clean anything around their house as the housekeeper and her employees took care of that. He wasn't all that messy, but the maid always cleaned his room too.

The holes were patched very quickly, and Captain Rigby started a game of football with the three younger ones. Connan decided to watch. He still didn't feel comfortable around them. He watched as they all ran back and forth across the yard. Dean did most of the tackling while Derek mainly stood around, watching for an opportunity to take the ball.

Connan heard a panting sound beside him and realized that the dog had laid down at his right side. Bailey watched him and licked the back of his hand. Connan reached up and stroked the dog's soft coat. *Something else I've never had, except at school . . .* Connan watched as Captain Rigby tackled Dean to the ground. He was perfectly content to sit with the dog. *Nothing shows just how lonely you are until you dive right into an actual family . . . They have so much, but with little.* Connan tried to focus more on Bailey to keep the gaping hole of loneliness at bay.

Tracy walked outside, letting the screen door slam. "Not playing with?"

Connan looked up at her as she came up behind him and Bailey. "Nah, not a big fan of football. I'm more of a gamer."

"Don't let Dean hear you say that." She sat down on the other side of Bailey. "He won't let you leave his room if he finds out."

"I'll keep that in mind." Connan didn't look at her. She was beautiful. Her long ginger hair moved with the breeze. Her petite frame had all the right curves a guy could ask for. Even her lips looked inviting. *Girls that can't control themselves enough to not stare is a no go ... too bad she can't. I bet she'd be a great kisser.*

"So ... ?" Tracy broke the silence. "What do you do for fun?"

"Spar." Connan responded. "Me and Daryn always . . ." He stopped himself. "We would spar every night. Otherwise, I play video games."

"Dean would probably spar with you." Tracy didn't seem to catch the last part. "Do you like to run?"

Connan rolled his eyes. *And there's the million-dollar question she's been dying to ask.* "No, something I am forced to do at school, won't be done while I'm home."

Tracy looked disappointed. "You probably don't like malls either . . . ."

Connan thought for a moment. "I like arcades . . . ."

"Would you want to go to the mall then? It has an arcade!" Tracy looked hopeful.

"Cap said your off limits."

"Eww, gross! That's not what I meant!" She wrinkled her nose.

"What, my abs not good enough for you?" Connan couldn't help but tease her now.

She rolled her eyes. "No, I already have a boyfriend. And you're really not my type anyway."

"What do you want then?" Connan looked over at her.

She sighed. "Dad won't let me go to the mall with Frank unless someone chaperones and I don't want Dean to come! He's a holy terror around Frank!"

"Frank your boyfriend?"

"Yes." She said smugly. "He's a great guy!"

"Yea, I bet he is." Connan looked back out at the yard. "Is there a computer store there?"

"Yeah, I think it's called 'PC Picnic' or something cheesy like that."

"Your boyfriend won't get jealous?"

"No, he doesn't get jealous."

Connan snorted. "All guys get jealous of other guys around their girls unless he's a player . . . Has he ever been in a fight?"

"No! He doesn't like violence." Tracy was red in the face.

Connan laughed. "Sure you want me to go?"

"Go where?" Captain Rigby held the football above his head and walked over to them. "You aren't going anywhere together."

"She wants me to chaperone her and her boyfriend instead of Dean." Connan snorted again trying to keep from laughing as Dean looked like he had just been hurt.

"But we always have such a blast with old Frankfort!" He stuck out his tongue at her.

"See! I don't want him ruining another date! Dad, please!"

"Frankfort?" Connan looked at Dean. "Why Frankfort?"

"Because!" Dean replied. "He's a big weenie!"

Connan laughed. "Guess that's better than what I was thinking."

"Don't you go there." Captain Rigby cut in.

"Sorry." Connan said while holding back his laughter.

"You're worse than Dean!" Tracy stomped back into the house.

"Hey, I didn't say anything!" Connan said while laughing.

"It was implied." Captain Rigby pointed a finger at him. "No perverted jokes, no matter how funny you think they are."

"Yes, sir." Connan couldn't keep a straight face as Dean had doubled over laughing.

"With that said, it would save Grace a trip if you went and got a few more pairs of clothes yourself. Do you have money to buy some new clothes?"

"Yea, I got money . . . Wait!" Connan stood up, startling Bailey. "You mean I have to go with her?"

"I think it would be a good experience for you. You can take Bailey with you. He has a service dog harness." Captain Rigby wasn't kidding. "He can keep you company while you watch her and Frank."

"Seriously?!" Connan was no longer laughing. "I literately have to watch her and her boyfriend? I haven't even been here a whole day and you're going to make me chaperone your daughter?"

"You can keep your distance, but I don't want her left alone. Not in this town. Once you're in the building, I don't care if you leave

Bailey with her and go do your own thing, but she's not walking there by herself."

"Don't have a choice in this either do I?" Connan glared.

"No."

Connan shook his head and went inside. Tracy was sitting on the couch. "What time were you supposed to be there?"

Tracy jumped. "Don't do that!" She put a hand on her chest. "You scared me half to death!"

"Just answer the question." Connan was getting more and more annoyed at her by the minute. "Cap said I have to take you. Bailey has to go too."

"Ugh! You better not embarrass me!"

"You do that on your own just fine, sweetheart!" Connan snapped. "What time?" Connan could tell he struck a nerve, but he really didn't care. *Didn't say I had to respect his daughter. Man, she's annoying!*

After she finally told him that she was supposed to eat lunch with him, he went and grabbed his wallet. He took out the credit cards that had his real name and his dad's name on them and replaced them with a chunk of the cash from the emergency envelope. He turned to leave and found Captain Rigby at his door.

"And you said you wouldn't fit in around here . . . No credit cards."

Connan handed Captain Rigby the cards he had taken out. "I'm not that stupid. Can you put them with my hard drive?"

Captain Rigby took the cards and went to leave. He stopped and turned back toward Connan. "I don't like this Frank guy. Of all the boys in the world, my baby girl had to go with a guy whose ego is too big for his own good. If he breaks her heart, do me a favor and break him."

Connan raised his eyebrows. "You're giving me permission to hurt this guy?" He shook his head. "First time I've ever been told I could do that!"

"She's my baby, Connan. Don't let her get hurt." Captain Rigby's tone had become softer. "Take good care of her."

"Can I at least make fun of them?"

"Have at it!" Captain Rigby smiled and disappeared from the doorway.

Connan closed his door and changed into the last set of clean clothes he had. *I smell like goats . . . Don't really want to take that to town. Still can't believe he would trust me to go to town, especially with his daughter. What if someone recognizes me from the pictures that are online? Daryn will find me for sure! I'll have to get a hat or something.*

Ten minutes later Tracy led the way up the road with Bailey at her side. She didn't talk to him. Connan preferred the silence as he didn't care much for talking. Especially to girls. *I hope I never get tangled up with a girl, no matter how pretty. They will just run off with other guys like Mom does to Dad.*

They made good timing as both were physically fit and wanted nothing more than to separate as soon as they got to the mall. Connan waited till Frank arrived before splitting. He found the computer place first. He bought a monitor and all the components he needed to build a small gaming computer. *Maybe Derek would help me.* He then made his way through several different clothing stores. He bought a ball cap while he was in a sporting goods store and immediately put it on. It made him feel much safer wearing a hat that concealed his features.

He found Tracy and Frank in the arcade once he finished his shopping. Frank was bragging about his skills on the shooting game. Connan leaned over Tracy's shoulder just to annoy her and force a reaction from her boyfriend. He laughed at Frank's final score. "You call that a good score?"

"Bet you can't do any better." Frank looked offended.

"Little sis here was holding back on you . . . I bet she could even destroy you if she didn't like you so much."

"Razor!" Tracy went red in the face.

"What? Only speaking truth!"

"Come on, Frank, he's just being annoying." Tracy tried to pull him away.

"Want to go a round?" Frank put a couple of quarters in the machine. "Put your money where your mouth is."

"No, he doesn't." Tracy's lips formed a thin line.

"Uh, yeah, I do." Connan smirked at Tracy and picked up the second gun. "Now watch how a master does it!"

Frank was completely defeated. He stared at Connan's high score. "How did you even do that?"

"Military school, my friend." Connan smiled. "Students aren't allowed the real thing, so we train with laser guns and games like this only on a military-grade level."

"Man, I don't think I could ever beat that high of a score!" Frank put the gun back in its place.

"Practice, lots of practice would help." Connan picked his shopping bags back up. "You two eat yet? I'm starved."

"You're not eating with us!" Tracy said, her jaw clenched. She put a hand on her hip. "Go eat somewhere else!"

"Come on, Tracy. Would it really be that bad if he joined us?" Frank gazed into her blue eyes. "I'm sure he won't mind tagging along. Besides, I have to skip after we eat. Dad's got me working in the garage with him after."

Tracy was speechless. She looked from Frank to Connan who smiled and flashed his eyebrows up and down as if to say, "I'm so going to ruin your date!" She stomped off leaving both boys shrugging their shoulders and running after her.

Connan found Frank a lot less egotistical than he thought he'd be. They talked about all the video games they played, and Frank was amazed that Connan could build a computer. Tracy, however, did not find Connan's company good at all. He had successfully hijacked her date.

After the boys had shook hands and Frank had given Tracy a kiss, they parted ways. Tracy fumed as they walked to the edge of the parking lot.

"You totally ruined my date!" She blurted out.

"Frank didn't think so." He smiled at her. "I gave you plenty of time while I got what I needed. Never said I couldn't crash the party."

This made her even more angry. "I'm so not talking to you ever again!"

"Kind of live in the same house so eventually you'll have to talk to me."

"I won't!"

"Uh . . . You just did."

"You're so immature!" Tracy stomped ahead of him after shoving Bailey's lead into his hands.

"Guess she wants to walk alone, doesn't she, Bailey?" Connan started after her. "Can't let her get too far ahead or Cap might kill me." He picked up his pace. A man cut in front of Tracy. Connan couldn't see what he was doing but Tracy had stopped and put her hands up.

He might have a gun! "Bailey, go!" He let go of the dog's leash as he had started barking wildly. The dog slowly approached his master's daughter and the man in front of her. Connan followed his lead and slowed as well. Tracy gave Bailey a command in German. The dog slowed but still growled and snarled at the man. Connan could see his hands now. *And he has a gun . . . great!*

"Just keep coming, kid!" The man turned the pistol toward Connan. "You're gonna hand over your wallet, nice and easy, or the girl gets it."

Connan slowly put his bags down as he studied the gun. "Just take it easy." He slowly and deliberately stepped in front of Tracy as he held his wallet out. The gun was oddly different from the guns he was used to seeing. "Bailey, attack!" Connan took a gamble and turned and shoved Tracy to the ground as Bailey lunged at the man, hitting him with all the force in his eighty-pound body. "Tracy, don't move! Call 911!" He pinned the man's flailing gun hand. Bailey was keeping him plenty busy so all he had to do was strip the gun.

"Tracy, call Bailey off!" He checked the gun's magazine to confirm his suspicions. "Tell Bailey to not let him move."

Bailey stood over the man snarling as the thief screamed in fear and pain. Tracy was on her feet and on the phone. Two minutes later two police officers rolled up and Captain Rigby drove up from the opposite direction. Connan handed over the gun as the officers took charge. The incident was starting to draw a crowd so Connan gave a statement to the officers as quickly as he could then hopped in the back of Captain Rigby's squad car. *I don't need this kind of attention on me! Daryn will see it and know exactly where to find me.* Tracy pulled open the back door on the opposite side and placed all of his bags in the seat.

"Thanks . . ." she said, voice shaking.

"Sorry for pushing you down." Connan could see she was shaken. "You alright?"

"Just a bit scared, but I'll be okay." She climbed in as Captain Rigby approached Connan's side. He opened the front door and Bailey jumped in. He then got into the driver's seat.

"You two alright?" He put the car into drive. "Not hurt, are you?"

"No," they answered.

It took five minutes to get home in the car. Captain Rigby let them out and they rushed inside. Tracy ran upstairs as fast as her feet would go, holding back the tears from the fright she had experienced. Connan gathered his bags and took them to his room. Captain Rigby followed after making sure Bailey had a sizable treat.

"Thank you for protecting my daughter." He glanced at the stairs. "This has never happened before."

"She's pretty scared." Connan sat down on the bed. "Bailey did all of the fighting."

"That may be, but I'm still very thankful you were there to help. If Dean would have gone . . . ."

"If he would've went, the worst that would have happened is they would've lost their money." Connan took a deep breath. "The guy didn't even have a bullet in the chamber. That was a Ruger, 9mm. Most of them have a little red bar that pops up if there's one in the chamber. I took the chance and had Bailey attack. I only stripped the gun. The mag was empty too."

"You noticed that?" Captain Rigby raised his eyebrows. "The gun was definitely empty. The guy must not have been too keen on hurting people."

"Kind of hard not to notice. The gun was lighter than it should've been. I will never test my running capabilities over Bailey's though. That's one thing I will never forget. That dog is fast!"

"Still, I'm glad you were there to protect my girl. Thank you."

"You're welcome." Connan smiled. "Is it okay if I show Derek how to put a computer together?"

"You bought a computer?"

"Only the parts, I have to build it. Figured it would be a good chance to see if Derek would communicate in that way."

Captain Rigby laughed. "And you didn't think you would fit in around here . . . You're acting like a real big brother."

Connan shrugged. "I may not have the world's best attitude, but I do like kids . . . for some odd reason . . . Not sure why, but I've always liked helping the younger cadets. That was the job I was offered at the academy for the summer. I was going to be a unit leader for the summer camps. We get elementary-age kids in for the summer and teach them survival skills."

John still smiled. "I think Derek would love to help."

9

GRACE WALKED IN as Connan started setting up his tools on the island alongside the computer parts. "Hey, I heard you and Tracy ran into some trouble on the way home from the mall. Are you two alright?" Worry etched the woman's face.

Man, Cap must tell her everything! Connan stopped what he was doing. "I'm fine. Tracy is pretty torn up about it. I'm pretty sure she's still crying. Not sure if it's because of the dude with the gun or because Frank likes me more than her now." He made his way around to the door. "Need any help with that?" *She seems really nice ... I'd help Hannah if she would let me.*

Grace nodded. "I see . . . There are more groceries in the trunk, if you really don't mind."

"I'll help!" Dean ran toward the door. "She's definitely crying about you stealing her date."

Connan couldn't help but laugh. Grace asked, "You stole her date? How?"

"I played a gun game with Frank and we hit it off. He invited me to eat with them." Connan grinned and opened the door. "She didn't like that he paid more attention to me at the table than to her!" He and Dean walked out the door laughing.

The two boys unpacked the rest of the groceries from the car for Grace. She had started putting everything away when she noticed Connan's tools and computer parts sitting on the island.

"What's all this for?" She asked as Connan and Dean brought the last of the groceries in.

"I went to that computer store in the mall and picked up all the parts for a gaming computer. Since I had to trash mine, I figured I might as well grab a new one. I thought Derek might like to help me put it together." Connan set the bags down then returned to the door to take his shoes off.

"That was very thoughtful of you to include Derek." Grace smiled. "I like the hat!"

Connan was still wearing the hat he'd picked up. "Thanks, figured it was best to keep my head covered if I go anywhere. Don't want anyone recognizing me from photos the news has put out."

"It's a very smart thing to do." Grace placed a jug of milk in the fridge. "Good news is the number of robberies has gone up around here, so your run in shouldn't go viral on the Web."

"I hope not." Connan sat down at the island. "When Daryn figures out I'm not going to the academy he'll be watching for anything and everyone that looks like me."

"Who's Daryn?" Dean started pulling items out of bags.

"He's a guy who currently hates me. So I'd rather not talk about him." Connan glanced up at Grace. She nodded and went back to putting the cold items in the fridge. Troy collected the bags as she emptied them.

Connan sat with Derek and Dean explaining the components of the computer and how to piece it together. Derek helped and even corrected Connan when he'd place something deliberately in the wrong spot. He could tell

Derek was soaking up every minute of the building process. *I'll have to get the stuff so Derek can build his own computer before I leave. He's got the brain capacity for it! I like these two. Grace is really nice... reminds me of Hannah. Hannah always took care of me!*

They spent the rest of the afternoon huddled around the computer. Connan could have pieced it together rather quickly, but he wanted to see if Derek would respond to such a thing. They finished as Grace had just finished cooking the taco meat for their dinner.

"Alright you three," She said. "I think it's time you go do your chores then wash up for dinner. Can we move the computer somewhere else, please?"

Connan carried his new computer to his room while the twins went to take care of the animals. The twins ran back in and straight to the bathroom to wash their hands. Tracy appeared to help set the table and James and Troy raced down the stairs with the captain at their heels. He stopped as Connan came out of his room.

"Any luck with Derek?" Captain Rigby asked in a whisper.

Connan smiled. "Worked like a charm. Doubt he talks but you may be able to understand him better through technology."

"I was hoping someone would be able to break the ice . . ." He paused and looked over at Tracy who kept slamming silverware down on the table. "Tracy, however, is not too happy."

"I can see that." Connan looked at her as she stomped away from the table to get the plates. "I didn't really mean to upset her. I was making fun of Frank's score on a gun game and he invited me to play . . . then he invited me to eat with them. She should be mad at him not me."

"That's not how she sees it. She sees it as you butting in on her date . . . and you can let her think that . . . don't argue." Captain Rigby could tell Connan wanted to defend his position. "Just let her be mad."

"Fine . . . She really doesn't have the right to be, but whatever." Connan separated from Captain Rigby and went to wash his hands as the other boys piled out of the bathroom.

Connan sat at the opposite end of the table this time. Since Tracy was home, the side chairs were taken. *At least I don't have to sit near her* . . . Connan helped himself to a taco salad and ate silently while the others conversed. Tonight wasn't any better. He still felt out of place. He had spent the day with the family for the most part and he had taken a liking to the twins. The family aspect still hurt . . . He ate as quickly as he could and asked to be excused.

"If it's alright, I'm going to go sit outside for a bit." Connan tried to communicate his uncomfortable state through his eye contact with Captain Rigby.

"Just don't do something stupid," the captain replied.

Connan just nodded and headed out the door. He didn't even bother putting his shoes on. *Why is dinner so hard for me? Nothing else has really bothered me. Probably because I see them as a family at the table, or maybe it's the whole praying thing. I've never had that kind of bond . . . even with Dad. Dad never prays, least of all to a god.* He sat down where he had the night before. He put his hand over his mouth where John had hit him. *Why does he care so much? I'm nobody to him* . . . He heard the door open.

"Razor?" Grace walked over to him and sat down beside him. "Is everything alright?"

"Yeah, I guess." Connan couldn't look at her. He didn't want to like Grace. *I've been hurt too many times; she'll eventually do the same!*

"Does sitting at the table with us bother you?" She didn't sound offended or hurt when she said this. "It's okay if you don't want to sit with us . . . I never sat with my foster parents for the first two months."

Connan looked over at her, surprised. "You were a foster kid?"

Grace nodded her head. "My father was in prison when I was born, and my mom couldn't care for me. The state took me from her."

"That's where we're different." Connan's bitterness was resurfacing. "I would leave my mom in a heartbeat without looking back . . . I had to run or die . . . At least your mom loved you."

Grace remained quiet for a few moments before getting up and turning toward the house. "I'm sorry you don't trust us, Razor. I can't promise you a joyful time while you're with us, but I can show you what love really means." She opened the door.

"Love? Never heard of it . . ." Connan let the bitterness out with every syllable. "I've never been loved like . . ." He trailed off, afraid he'd upset her and have to face the captain. "I'm fine, just need to be alone for a few." He heard the door close softly behind Grace as she reentered the house.

Grace couldn't help but tear up. Her husband met her inside the door. "What's wrong? If he said something to hurt you, I'll . . . ."

"John," Grace shook her head. "It's not what he said . . . well it is what he said, but he . . . John, he doesn't know what love truly means. I don't think he can even process it. That's why he can't sit at the table. He sees us all together, and he's never had that before. John, he's never had a family, let alone a mother who loves him." She let the tears flow but kept her voice low. "I feel so terrible for him . . . I wish I knew how to comfort him, but he doesn't trust me. I don't think he trusts anyone. How are we supposed to help him?"

John wrapped his wife in his arms. "I don't know, Grace. He's lost, but no one is beyond God's reach . . . Patience may be the best thing right now. Be patient and love him from a distance. It takes a lot of courage to leave a full-time nursing position like you did to take on the role of a foster parent . . . To love your children, even the ones that aren't blood related, is a hard job when they have a background like his."

John held his wife until Troy started yelling from the dinner table. Grace went to him immediately and John looked out the front door's window. He watched as Connan buried his head in his hands. *Lord, we may not know how to help at the moment, but you do. Send him help, Lord, send him help.* John jumped as Bailey trotted passed him and out the dog door. The dog paused when he saw Connan on the stairs then slowly stalked toward him. He padded down the stairs then turned and sniffed at Connan's hands.

John watched in amazement as Bailey forced his way between Connan's knees and hands till Connan wrapped him into a hug. "I'll be darned." Captain Rigby smiled and silently thanked Jesus. He walked back to the table and picked up his and Connan's plates. He took them to Grace who now stood over the sink. "I think he will be just fine," he whispered to her. "God's got it all covered."

A few moments later, Connan walked back in with Bailey trailing him. "If you don't care, I'm going to go to bed." After a quick nod from Captain Rigby, Connan went straight to his room. He changed into a pair of sweats he had picked up at the mall and transferred his new computer from the bed to his dresser. Once he laid down, Bailey jumped up on the bed with him. The dog curled up at his feet and watched him, keeping a constant vigil over him.

Grace and John silently opened his door a bit wider when they themselves headed toward bed. "I asked God to send the boy some help," John whispered. "Next thing I know, Bailey walks out the front door and forced him to pay attention to him. It took a few seconds for Connan to realize what Bailey wanted, but I never saw someone become so attached so quickly to something... He may never trust a human, but a dog will never betray him."

John pulled the door back to its cracked position. Bailey would need room to get out if he had to. John thought it highly unlikely the dog would move all night. He got up early the next morning to check and he found Bailey stretched out next to Connan. Connan had his arm wrapped around the dog's chest.

"Bailey," John called. Bailey swung his head around, his ears forward. The sudden movement woke Connan. "Morning," John said.

"Thought you might like to get to the bathroom before the morning rush."

Connan nodded his head still half asleep. "Thanks." He sat up on the side of the bed with his back to the door. Bailey hopped off the bed and headed for the door. The dog looked back to make sure Connan was following. When Connan didn't move, Bailey went to him and nudged him with his nose.

Connan rubbed the sleep from his eyes. Bailey nudged him again. "I'm okay, Bailey." He yawned. "I'm coming." Bailey sat down and waited for him. John called Bailey to him, but the dog refused to move. He whined when John called to him again.

"Well, I think you're his favorite person now . . . It was Derek, but now he won't even leave your side." John almost laughed. "He thinks you're his now."

Connan patted the dog on the head before standing up. John was right. As Connan walked to the bathroom, Bailey followed. When Connan closed the door on him, the dog started to whine and scratch at the door till John commanded him in German to go outside. Connan was finishing up when he heard a yelling match break out upstairs. He opened the door and found Tracy waiting for him to get out. Again, she stared at his bare chest.

Connan couldn't help himself. "What, didn't get a good enough view yesterday?" He flexed.

"Oh my gosh." Tracy put her hands over her eyes. "Put a shirt on!"

"Get used to it, sweetheart... Or beat Dean to the bathroom next time." Connan grinned and slid past her. "What?" John was looking at him over his reading glasses.

"Sweetheart?" He asked.

Connan grinned. "She doesn't like when I call her that... Just trying to make her dislike me as much as possible... You said she was off limits so if I can't date her, I'll harass her like Dean does."

"I wouldn't date you if you were the last boy on earth!" Tracy stepped into the bathroom.

"Mission complete!" Connan flexed at her again.

She slammed the door closed. Connan looked back over at the captain. "Was that too much?"

"Borderline..." John replied. "I don't think a boy your age has ever done that to her. She doesn't know how to react other than thinking you are completely immature."

"Well, this way, she will avoid me. Though I may see if I can't plan a hangout day with Frank."

"You think Frank is that cool, do you?" John put his Bible down.

"Don't you dare!" Tracy yelled from the other side of the bathroom door. "Stay away from him! I don't want you corrupting him!"

"See, now I have to hang with Frank!" Connan laughed.

"Go get dressed." John snorted, trying to hold back his own outburst of laughter. "I'll get his number to you later."

"Dad, no!" came a shout from the bathroom.

10

"WOULD YOU, BOYS, leave her alone?" Grace came down the hall.

Connan went back to his room to finish dressing and John went back to reading his Bible. Breakfast was fried bologna and toast. Tracy sat sulking as everyone else kept up a conversation. Dean sat nearest to Connan so they could talk about video games. Connan kept glancing up at Tracy. She looked angry but kept her temper under control. He could hardly believe how well she could keep her tongue in check.

Connan helped the boys with feeding and Bailey followed them all over the yard. Connan couldn't help but feel a little bad for teasing Tracy so much. He picked up a stick and tossed it for Bailey to fetch. *I'll have to make it up to her somehow.* He liked her and didn't want her to stay mad at him. *Maybe we could make up and call a truce.* Connan tried to find a good time throughout the day to get her alone. No opportunity presented itself until early evening.

"Dad, would you run with me? Dean refused." Tracy tied her shoes.

"Hun, I am leaving for work in a half hour, I don't have the time. We should've ran this morning." John was heading to his bedroom. "Ask Razor."

"I'll go." Connan shut down his computer. He and Derek had just finished installing its firewalls. "Let me change real fast."

Tracy rolled her eyes but didn't object. Five minutes later they were walking down the drive with Bailey at their heels. Once they stepped up their pace from a walk to a slow run, Connan started in.

"Tracy?" She didn't answer. "Can we talk, please? I feel terrible for teasing you. Would you please talk to me?"

"You should feel bad!" Tracy picked up her pace as if to out distance him.

"Tracy," Connan smiled "You can't outrun me . . . I do this every morning during the school year." He caught up and matched her pace. "Look, I'm sorry I teased you. Can we please call a truce? I don't like you being mad at me . . . It bothers me for some reason."

"So the big bad boy does have a heart." Tracy sneered. "You barely know me, and you start acting like Dean! I can't catch a break between the two of you!"

"I said I was sorry!" Connan grabbed her arm and made her stop. "I'll lay off, can we please be friends?"

"I've never had an older brother." Tracy avoided his eyes. "I thought you'd be more mature than a thirteen-year-old."

"Dean and Derek are only three years younger than us . . . When's your birthday?"

"November, why?"

"I'm only eight months older than you. I've never had siblings, let alone a sister . . . I'm sorry I messed up your lunch date yesterday. If I hang with Frank, I'll make sure it's when you two don't have plans and if Cap asks me to chaperone again, I'll stay away. Sound fair?"

Tracy sighed and started walking again. "I guess . . . Thanks for apologizing."

The rest of their run was more pleasant. By the time they had returned, John had left for his twenty-four-hour shift at the station and Grace had started supper. Tracy went straight to the shower and Connan helped Derek with the animals as Dean was asked to set the table. By the time they got back in, Tracy had finished her shower and Connan was able to get his. After everyone had gone to bed, Connan snuck into the living room and grabbed John's Bible. *I gotta find that story . . . .*

The Rigby household was starting to get used to their new family member and Connan was finding it easier and easier to sit through dinner. As the days rolled into weeks, he accepted the family more and more. He kept his teasing of Tracy to a minimum so she wouldn't get too mad at him. Frank turned out to be a good friend and Grace relied more and more on him. In just a few weeks, Connan had picked up chores like the rest of the kids. He emptied the trash for Grace and would help babysit when Grace went out. He helped with the animals and took over Bailey's care. Bailey stayed by his side as much as possible.

Connan would stay home when the family went to church. He didn't feel comfortable in a church setting. It was during another twenty-four-hour shift for John when Grace called him late at night.

"John," she cried. "He called me Mom!" She tried to keep her voice from shaking. "He . . . Razor called me . . . Oh, John!"

Captain Rigby was silent. He couldn't believe what he was hearing. Razor, Connan Hyatt, had just called his wife Mom. "He actually said Mom?"

"Yes, John. We were finishing dinner and I had started collecting plates and he said 'Thanks, Mom.' I think it surprised him as much as it surprised me! He tried to avoid me the rest of the evening. Of course Bailey was trying to herd him, so he finally joined me for a movie with Troy!"

"I'll be darned . . . Sounds like he's took his next step in learning to trust you."

Grace talked well into the night with her husband. Her excitement would not let her sleep. Connan was in the same boat. He couldn't sleep. *I can't believe I let that slip! It was so weird . . . I've never had a mom like her . . . It really felt strange, but good at the same time! What if after all this business with Daryn is over, I don't want to go home? I have to accept that I will have to go home . . . If he doesn't kill me.*

Connan's worries had faded by morning. He was up before anyone and read a little more out of the book of Luke before anyone got up. He marked his place as he had the last time John was on shift. He had planned to go to the mall with Dean. Frank would be meeting them at the arcade. Connan thought they could go early and pick up the parts for another computer for Derek to build. He also needed a new pair of running shoes. He and Tracy had made it their routine to get up early and go run. He was now her coach for the remainder of the summer.

After chores and breakfast, Connan and Dean headed out with Bailey. The others would be making rice crispy treats with Grace while they were gone. Dean took him to a comic bookstore before they went to the mall. He showed him his favorites and Connan let him pick one out for himself and Derek. He grabbed a few for his collection too. When they entered the mall, they hurried their shopping so they could eat before meeting Frank.

They finished their shopping early and headed for the cafeteria. "Dang it! I forgot my hat!" Connan started looking around for the closest store.

"Eh, no one cares if you . . ." Dean pulled on Connan and hid behind a large pillar.

"Hey! What's that about?" Connan followed Dean's pointing finger.

"Is that Frankfort?" Dean asked. "Who's the girl?"

Connan's anger started to rise. "It better be his sister." Connan made his way across the cafeteria. "Hey, buddy!"

Frank jumped. "Razor! What are you doing here so early?" He began to sweat. "Didn't think I'd be seeing you guys till later!"

"You didn't tell me you had a sister! Can I get her number?" Connan had him cornered.

"Sister?" The girl put a hand on her hip. "I'm his girlfriend."

Connan crossed his arms over his chest. He looked ready to kill. "That's funny, because I thought my sister was his girlfriend."

Frank swallowed hard as the girl started cussing him out. Connan stopped her. "You seem like a nice girl, but may I?" The girl stomped off yelling, "It's over Frank!"

"You're a real piece of work, you know that?" Connan got in his face. Dean tried to pull Connan away, but Connan wouldn't budge. "You know if Dean wasn't here, I'd bash your face in!" Connan turned to leave. "Hell, if I won't!" He turned back around and punched him square in the jaw. "Stay away from Tracy! Come on, Dean." Connan walked away shaking his hand and leaving Frank sprawled on the floor.

When they arrived home, Grace had just started on making the treats. "Your home early!"

"Frank canceled." It's all Connan could get out without blurting out that Frank was a downright cheater and that he had given him what he deserved. "Probably a good thing. Looks like it could rain soon." He was still fuming and could tell Grace knew something was wrong. He tried to pretend otherwise. *I've never been a good liar . . . She won't buy it.*

Dean didn't say anything and followed Connan to his bedroom. "Did you see the look on his face when you decked him! I still can't believe you did that!" Dean kept his voice to a whisper. "You really scared me, Razor. I don't think I've ever seen you that mad before . .

." A chill raced up Dean's spine, making him shiver.

"Sorry, Dean . . . I didn't mean to upset you. The jerk got what he deserved." Connan fumed. "I really didn't mean to scare you, bud. I haven't got that mad since Dad said I couldn't take the summer job at the academy."

"His face though when we walked over!" Dean burst out laughing. "I thought I was going to die! He probably thought so too!"

Connan snorted. "Don't tell Tracy . . . I don't want to hurt her."

"I don't either . . ." Dean stuck a finger in his ear. "Want to give Derek his computer?"

"Later tonight," Connan replied "Let's see if Mom needs another couple of hands. Maybe we can sneak a couple bites!"

They made their way back to the kitchen island where the others were gathered. They joined in and soon forgot about their run in with Frank. Tracy had disappeared upstairs. Grace kept eyeing them. Connan had just put a small clump of the treat mix in his mouth when Tracy stormed back down the stairs. She grabbed him by the arm and pulled him toward the door. He grabbed his shoes before she could pull him outside.

She slammed the door. "You hit Frank! I can't believe you!"

"He called you?" Connan crossed his arms. "What did the jerk say?"

"Said you just walked up and punched him for no reason! He broke up with me because of you!"

"Good! He's not good enough for you! And that's not what happened!" Connan could hardly control his anger now. "He better stay away from you and you better stay away from him!"

"You can't tell me what to do and you're the real jerk! Why would you hit him! Frank is kind and loves me!" Tracy started to yell.

"Is that what he's been telling you? That he loves you?" Connan got in her face. "He doesn't love anyone but himself! He'll be sorry forever . . . ."

"I hate you!" She screamed. "I hate that you even came here! You've ruined everything!" Tears ran down her face.

Her words stung. He took her by the arms and pulled her close. "I didn't ask to be here," he said in a low, dangerous tone. "I didn't ask for any of this. We caught him with another girl, Tracy. He's been cheating on you." He let go of her, slipped his shoes on, and walked off down the drive. Bailey ran after him.

"What?" Tracy whispered to herself. "No, he . . . Frank wouldn't do that!" She ran inside and turned Dean around. Her tears were streaming down her face. "What happened at the mall? And don't lie!" She was almost in hysterics.

"Tracy?" Grace tried to intervene.

Tracy stopped her. "I need to know what you saw, Dean. Tell me!"

Dean's shoulders dropped. "You really want to know? We saw Frank with another girl. Razor thought it may have been his sister or something so he went and asked Frank if he could get her number. The girl with him said she was his girlfriend . . . Razor told her that he thought that was funny because his sister was actually Frank's girlfriend. The girl started cussing him out and Razor told her to get lost. Then he punched Frank."

"No! He wouldn't do that to me! Frank loves me!" Tracy fell to her knees. "He said he loved me!"

Grace went over and helped her stand. "Go find Razor," she said to Dean as she hugged Tracy around the shoulders and took her up to her room. Dean put on his shoes and went outside. He started calling for Connan. The rain had started coming down. Connan didn't answer and he started to panic. He ran around the edge of the yard yelling for him and even looked in the donkey's shelter. When he couldn't find him, he ran back inside and up the stairs.

"Mom! Mom! Razor's gone! I can't find him!" Dean panted at his sister's door. "Mom, he's gone!"

"Oh, no!" Tracy wailed even louder. "It's all my fault! I told him I hated him!" She cried into Grace's shoulders.

Grace looked at Dean. "Oh, Lord, I pray he didn't go far!" She thought for a moment. "Call your dad and tell him what happened. I need to stay here with your sister. He's on patrol duty today, so call Meg over at dispatch to get a hold of him. And, Dean, hurry. I don't want him getting hurt!"

"Okay!" Dean rushed back down the stairs with Tracy sobbing, "I hurt him so bad, Mom!" He grabbed the home phone off its charger and dialed 911.

"Nine-one-one, what's your emergency?"

"I need to talk to Meg! This is Dean!"

"Oh, hey, Dean, This is Meg. What's up, bud?"

"Tell Dad Razor left!"

"The new kid?"

"Yeah! He left like five or ten minutes ago! I can't find him!"

"I'll let him know ASAP." Meg disconnected the call and pushed a button that connected her directly to Captain Rigby. "Captain, your son Dean just called . . . He needed you to know that your new foster kid, Razor, has ran away. They can't find him . . . ."

"Put me out on call till I get back with you. Thanks, Meg." John hung up the phone and turned his lights and sirens on. *Lord Jesus, don't let him get far!* He headed straight for the house. He pulled in and found Dean waiting for him. Dean hopped in the back and John took off again. "What happened? Why'd he run?"

"When we were at the mall we caught Frank with another girl. Razor punched him and Frank ended up calling Tracy and breaking up with her. Tracy said she told Razor that she hated him . . . We couldn't find him after that."

"I knew that flake was no good! I'll have to have a word with Frank's father." John reeled out of the driveway heading away from town. "Connan wouldn't go toward town . . . If he had, I would've seen him."

"Connan?" Dean raised his eyebrows. "I thought we were looking for Razor."

"We are, his real name is Connan, and you're not going to tell anyone that! If someone finds out his real name, he will be in terrible danger . . . Did you see him before he took off?"

"No, sir, but I think Bailey is with him. I couldn't find him either. Is that why Razor wears a hat every time he goes out?"

"That's a good sign . . . He may just be blowing off steam. And yes, he doesn't want anyone to recognize him. The story and his picture were all over the news when he arrived here." John slowed his car down. "If he came this way, we should see him directly."

11

"**D**AD!" DEAN POINTED up ahead. A very familiar German Shepherd sat watching the road. John turned his lights on. "Dean, stay in the car, the rain is picking up." He stepped out of the car and Bailey came toward him.

"Where is he, boy?" John followed the dog deeper into the wood line. He started hearing indistinct shouting. *Is he shouting at . . . God?* John slowed. He hid behind a large tree just outside of Connan's vision. He listened.

"Why? If there really is a God then find me! I always take the fall! If you are there, just say something! Anything!"

John watched as Connan punched a tree. "Aagh!" He shook his hand. He went to punch the tree again, but John rushed forward and grabbed his arm. His right hand was bloody.

Not him! Not now! "What do you want?" Connan fought the urge to punch the man as he jerked out of his grip.

"I got a call saying you had run off." John kept a cool tone. He couldn't decide whether to feel sorry for Connan or be angry with him.

"I wanted to be alone. Of course, the stupid dog followed me . . . Grace call you?"

"Dean did," John took out a handkerchief. "Give me your hand." He wrapped his handkerchief around Connan's bloody knuckles. "They got worried when you disappeared."

"Figures," Connan replied in a huff. "Should've known I wouldn't be able to get away for even a few minutes!"

"Calm down." John was now becoming more angry than he was sorry for him. He stayed calm, hoping Connan wouldn't lash out at him physically. *He's a fighter, I don't want to provoke him.*

"Calm down? What, no morality speech? I hate this place! I can't catch a break! I start to care for anything and anyone and I get stabbed in the back!" Connan kept his rant going. "I caught that slimy piece of trash with another girl and how am I repaid? She cuts me! Why do I even try to help? I always get hurt! I get the brunt of everything! Always have! I should've never trusted her!"

"Are you done?"

"Yeah, I think so...."

"Feel any better?" John asked.

"No," came the reply. "I was angry, so I punched the stupid jerk. Told him to never come around again. Then she hits me harder than I ever hit Frank!"

"I thought you said you were done?" John cocked his head. "Let it all out, son."

"I'm not your son," Connan said in a lower tone.

"No, but as long as you're under my roof I will treat you as I do my sons. Let's get out of this rain." John started back toward his patrol car. "Grace will be worried sick if I don't get you back soon."

Connan followed. He tried to ignore the "son" part of John's words. *He wishes... By the way he's talking, I probably wouldn't get away with yelling at him if I were.* The patrol car came into view and Dean had his nose pressed up against the back driver window. He smiled when he saw Connan.

"Get in, and no arguments." John let Bailey into the back seat then climbed into the driver seat.

Yea, he's definitely mad. Connan slowly went around the car and got in the passenger seat. He caught John telling Dean not to give him any grief. They rode in silence back to the house. Connan and Captain Rigby waited on the porch as Dean ran in to get them towels.

"You best apologize to Grace for running off like that . . . She's probably worried sick."

Connan just nodded a reply. He didn't feel like talking anymore. Dean ran back out and gave each of them a towel before rubbing Bailey down. Grace walked out a few seconds later.

"Thank you, John." She looked at Connan. "Go get dried off. I laid some clothes out for you." Her voice was shaking and she was on the verge of crying.

Her words weren't harsh, but Connan could tell she was angry with him. "Yes, Ma'am." *I don't know what hurts worse . . . Tracy's words or the fact I've hurt Grace.* Connan went inside. He felt crushed by the look Grace had given him.

I really worried her . . . He held back tears as he made his way to the bathroom.

"What was he thinking?" Grace was in tears. "He had me worried sick! Tracy shouldn't have said she hated him, but he should've never ran off like that!"

"He needs help, and I will be having a talk with him once I'm off duty. May need to wrap his hand. He punched a tree several times by the look of it . . . Unrelated, but have you been reading my Bible?"

Grace wrinkled her forehead. "No, why?"

"I keep finding bent pages . . . You know I like to keep the pages straight . . . I wonder if Connan's been reading and doesn't want anyone to know . . . ."

"He's been getting up the last couple weeks before anyone else. I thought it was to beat the bathroom rush. Do you think he is learning anything?"

"I think it could be angering him since he has no guidance in it. Grace, he was yelling at God in the woods down the road . . . ."

"Do you think he would talk to us about it?"

"Not likely . . ." John shook his head. "He's hurting at the moment. I need to call Meg and get back. Make sure he stays put."

"I'll make sure he doesn't go anywhere before you get back. Thank you for getting him."

John kissed his wife. "You're welcome. He better apologize to you . . . I really need to get back in service, so I'll talk to you later." He wrapped the towel around her and gave her a hug. He then ran to his car and ducked inside.

Grace was waiting for Connan in the living room when he came out of the bathroom. She stood and faced him. He waited to see if she would say anything. She didn't. *She looks really disappointed in me* . . . .

He took a step toward her. "I . . . ."

She held a hand out up to stop him. She took a deep breathe. "Why?"

"Frank deserved . . ." Grace cut him off.

"Not that. Why did you run away? Razor, running from your problems won't solve anything!" She held back more tears.

"I . . . I'm sorry, Mom. I really didn't mean to hurt you. I just wanted to be alone." He swallowed hard as a tear ran down Grace's cheek.

She closed the distance and wrapped him in a hug. "Don't ever scare me like that again, you hear me." She kissed him on the cheek. "I was so worried about you!"

"I'm sorry, Mom," Connan repeated, tears streaming down his face. "It won't happen again."

"Yes, it will." Grace held him at arm's length. "All teens need to blow off steam every once in a while. Next time, tell me where you are going, okay?" She wiped the tears from his eyes. Connan nodded.

"Razor?" Tracy stood at the bottom of the stairs. Troy hid behind her and James peeked out from the staircase. She took a couple of steps forward when Connan didn't respond. "I . . ." She couldn't get the rest out. She ran back upstairs crying.

Grace waved at the others and they disappeared back upstairs. "She's a complete mess. Once she heard what had happened from Dean, she lost it all together." Grace made him look at her. "She could really use a big brother right now."

Connan shook his head. "I . . . I can't! She hurt me as much as the truth hurt her . . . different pain, same severity. I can't just . . ." He sighed. *Stop with the sad blue eyes!* "Fine, I'll go up there. Don't think it will do a bit of good though."

Grace gave him half a smile and let go of his shoulders. "You are such a good brother."

Connan huffed. "I'll try to be as long as I'm here." He walked toward the stairs with his hands in his pockets.

"That's my boy." Grace said under her breath. *Lord, guide him!*

Connan took the stairs one at a time as slowly as he could. He had till he reached Tracy's door to be mad at her, so he went as slowly as possible. *I really don't want to make up right now. I don't even want to see her! I'm only doing this for Grace.* Connan pushed her door all the way open. He had never been in her room. *She's way messier than the twins put together.* She sat on the window seat with her knees drawn up to her chest and her head buried between her arms.

Connan sat down by her feet. He felt sorry for her in that moment. He gently pushed her feet off the seat and scooted closer to her. He wrapped his arm around her, giving her a side hug. She leaned into him and wrapped her arms around him.

"I'm so sorry, Razor, I didn't mean it! I didn't mean it!" She cried even harder when Connan placed his other arm around her.

"I'm sorry too." Connan rested his chin on the top of her head. "If it makes you feel any better, I laid Frank out on the floor. The other girl didn't know he had a girlfriend."

Tracy shook her head against his chest. "I don't care about that! I hurt you, Razor . . . I'm so sorry!"

Connan just held her. They sat like this until Tracy ran out of tears. She sat up and wiped her face. Connan let go of her. He still felt burned, but he was no longer mad at her. He stood up and went to leave. Tracy grabbed his right hand.

"Oh, Razor, what did you do?" Blood still oozed from the wounds on his knuckles. Tracy stared at it.

"I punched a tree . . . more than once . . ." He shook his hand out of hers and went to her bedroom door. He closed it so none of the little ones could listen in. He sat back down beside her. "All my life, I've been pushed aside. My mom never wanted me, Dad's never around, and my best friend was my bodyguard." He lowered his voice. "Tracy, I'm the kid from the news . . . I'm Connan Hyatt . . . I'm the one that discovered the plot to kill my dad and my best friend is now trying to get to me because he was in on it."

Tracy stared wide eyes at him. He kept on. "I have never been wanted. That's why I left. You cut me deep. This is the only place I have felt like I halfway belong. Once Daryn is caught I'll have to return to my life. A single child, neglected by his own parents . . . that's why it hurt. If I was anyone else, I would've just shrugged it off like you were on your . . . Well, never mind." He stared at the floor, a bit embarrassed.

"Oh, Razor . . . Connan." Tracy leaned on his shoulder. "I'm sorry. I do want you here. I want you to stay. Dad won't bash Frank's face in and Dean's too young. I'm glad I have an older brother who's looking out for me."

"I will always protect those around me. It's part of the Marine Code at the academy. As long as I'm here, I'll bash anyone's face in who tries to hurt you."

This made Tracy laugh. "Just don't scare all the boys away."

"I'm sure I'll approve of a few . . . if I'm still around." Connan stood up. "Should probably open the door before the boys start building stories. Don't say anything about who I really am. For one, Cap would kill me and we don't want it leaked and Daryn end up finding me."

"I won't . . . I like the name Razor. It suits you." Tracy looked out the window. "Looks like Dad got off early. He's pulling in the drive."

"Oh, joy. He's probably still mad at me. Mom wasn't very happy with me either . . . I really worried her." Connan opened the door.

"She really loves you as her own. Mom loves, and it shows in everything she does." Tracy kept her eyes focused on the car pulling up to the house. "She worries about you as much as she does the rest of us."

Connan left her there and reluctantly made his way downstairs. Grace was emptying the trash in the kitchen, so he sped up. "Let me do that."

Grace stood up straight. "Thank you . . . not trying to butter me up, are you?" she squinted at him with an eyebrow raised.

"No. Just thought I'd save Cap from having to yell for me." Connan pulled the full bag out. "He just pulled in."

"I see. Did you and Tracy . . . ?"

"We're good." Connan tied the bag shut and headed for the front door. He could tell she had just been crying. Her face was flushed and her eyes were puffy. "You can call this a head start on all the chores I'll have to do now."

"John was definitely not happy with you." Grace gave him an "I'm sorry" smile.

John opened the front door as Connan reached for the knob. "Just who I wanted to talk to." Connan pulled his boots on then stepped outside with the trash. "What's this? Trying to appease Grace?"

"No, sir," Connan replied. "Thought I'd get a head start on the chores you're going to make me do."

John crossed his arms. "You really think extra chores are going to amend you running off like that?"

"No," Connan closed the door. "Dad would have kicked my butt. You don't seem to be the type to do that except at your job, so I figured I'd end up doing more chores or something."

"You ran off, Connan." John started walking up the drive. Connan followed right behind him. The rain had all but stopped. "Dean was panicked, Grace was worried sick, and I had half a mind to take a belt to you . . . Extra chores." John shook his head. Connan threw the trash in a large bin at the end of the drive.

He turned to go back toward the house but the captain stopped him. "Connan, if you were my boy, I would take a belt to you, but you aren't mine. And I am not going to overstep my bounds when your dad should do the disciplining. What am I supposed to do? What can I do?"

Connan shook his head. "Ask Dad . . . He'd probably tell you to use a belt. I'd rather be whipped than see Grace so upset again."

John closed his eyes and took a deep breath. "Running off like that is one of the stupidest things you could've done." He shook his head. "Come on . . . Grace will think I've killed you if we don't get back. Did you apologize to her?"

Connan nodded his head. "Yeah, I'm sorry you had to come after me. It won't happen again."

"It better not. You've never had a consistent parent influence, have you?"

"No," Connan walked beside John back to the house. "It's nice having that here . . . even when I'm asked to do something I don't want to do . . . Grace made me make up with Tracy." Connan stepped up on the porch. "One of the hardest things I've had to do for her . . . I will never forget the way she looked at me."

Connan hung his head, not wanting to look at the captain. "No one's ever gone after me like that, or loved me enough to care."

"Needless to say, I don't think you will do that again if you truly couldn't stand Grace being upset with you." John opened the door. "I still have half a mind to take my belt to you." Connan didn't reply. He walked in the house and took his boots off. He went to sit down at the island, but John stopped him. "Oh no, you don't. You can spend the rest of the evening in your room; and no computers."

Connan turned to protest but saw Grace give him a "Don't test him" look so he thought better of it. "Yes, sir." He stuffed his hands in his pockets and crossed the dining and living rooms. He made a quick stop in the bathroom then went to his room. He went to close the door then picked up his computer. He took it out and set it in front of Captain Rigby on the island.

"If it's in there, I'll be on it." He turned and went back to his room.

"At least, he's being honest." Grace whispered. "Are you sure you're not being too harsh?"

"Would you rather me use a belt on the boy?" John picked up the computer. "Grace, he has to learn, and violence is all he knows. Taking another route may be more beneficial. I'm going to put this in the office and get changed." John stalked off, leaving Grace looking after him.

12

Connan stayed in his room all evening. John sat in the living room where he could see the door to his bedroom.

"Should I fix him a plate?" Grace held a plate up. "John, does Razor get any supper?"

"Fix him one, I'll take it to him." He stood and went to the island. Tracy was helping set the table.

"Daddy, it's all my fault. I told him . . . ."

"He still ran off, Tracy. It doesn't matter what was said, it matters how he reacted." John looked at her. "The only thing he did do right today was stop Frank from ever calling on you again."

"But, Daddy! He said he was sorry! Why can't he join us?"

"Enough," John replied. "He is confined to his room for the night and that's the end of it." Grace handed him a plate and he left the kitchen.

John knocked on Connan's door before entering. Connan sat on the edge of bed closest to the door. He held the burner phone in his hand.

John sat the dinner plate down on the nightstand. He paused, then turned to leave.

"Wait. Please." Connan stood. "I should've given this to you. I haven't used it since I first got here and sent Dad a text telling him I was safe. I keep it turned off, but it's the only thing I have that's connected to my dad." It's got his number on redial if you ever need to call him . . . It's untraceable. Daryn can't track it."

"I could've used this earlier this afternoon . . . thank you for being honest with me." John took the phone and left the room.

Connan sat the plate outside his door when he had finished. He didn't dare disobey the captain. *I don't mind being in here all night. They really care about me . . . I hurt Mom so this is deserved.* He laid across the bed and stared out the window. *I don't like this kind of discipline though . . . Dad would kick me around a bit then call it good. I won't forget this . . . I've never been in trouble and not been able to fight back. Guess that's the difference between someone who has to care and someone who genuinely cares. I wish Cap was my dad.*

John unlocked his office. He sat behind his desk and turned the phone over and over. Grace came in the door. "Supper is on the table." She looked at the phone. "Is everything alright?"

John held up the phone. "Connan gave this to me . . . said it's the only connection to his dad. He hasn't used it since he first arrived." John took a deep breath. "Grace, I have been tempted to call him up and deal with Connan through him; but something keeps telling me I handled the situation better than Mr. Hyatt could've."

"You told me earlier, he was used to violence. John is there any way we could just adopt him?" Grace leaned on the door frame. "He's been through so much and I wish it would stop with us. He needs stability and if he goes back to Denver . . . I don't want to think of how he would grow up in that environment."

"We could possibly transfer guardianship, but he'll be eighteen in a little under two years. He's already had a lot of bad influence in his life, and we are still processing the adoption of Derek, Dean, and James. After that was Troy . . . I don't know how much more the state would allow us to fully adopt our foster kids? It's hard enough trying to adopt the three and the state is dragging their feet."

"I know, but their parents aren't alive anymore . . . Troy's mom signed over guardianship to us, we just have to set the court date to make it official. Now, you have a direct line to Connan's father. We just have to pray about it and ask God for guidance."

John stood up, leaving the phone on his desk. "You're right . . . Who knows how long it will take for all this to blow over with Connan? He could be here till he's eighteen. If we have another incident like this, I will call. That way I will have full blessing to treat him as my own son." John relocked his office and went to the dinner table with his wife. "That way I can sentence him to hard labor."

Over the next week, Connan found that he and Tracy had gotten closer. John hadn't grounded him, so they still went on morning runs. One morning, he found Tracy pleading with Grace.

"But, Mom, it's not like if we see him Razor will kick his face in. One time was enough, and Frank hasn't called or anything!"

"Tracy, last time he was at the mall, he hit someone! I'm not taking that chance!" Grace continued down to the basement to start a load of laundry. "Besides, your dad said no mall trips for a while without supervision from one of us."

Connan hurried out and waited with Tracy till Grace reappeared. "Come with us! I need a new pair of running shoes if Tracy and I are going to keep running together."

"Not you too!" Grace poured a basket of clean clothes out on the couch. "I have a lot to get done today!"

"We will help!" Tracy said as she bounced on her heels. "Please, Mom!"

Grace straightened up and put both hands on her hips. "If you really want to go then here's what needs done." She held up a hand. "One, rooms need cleaned and I'm not saying stuff your closet and stash things under the bed. Two, dishes need done. Three, bathrooms need cleaned. Four, laundry has to be done and put away. And, all needs done before I have to take Troy to his doctor's appointment in two hours. There's also trash, and the floors need swept and mopped."

"We can do that!" Tracy headed for the basement. "I'll start on the bathrooms!"

"I'll go help the boys clean up their rooms." Connan turned toward the stairs.

"What, saving your room till last? Are you really that messy?" Tracy teased.

"No, my room is clean." He gave her a cheesy grin. "Unlike you, I am used to making my bed every morning, and making sure dirty clothes actually get into the laundry bin." He ran up the stairs to avoid her piercing glare.

Two hours later, they were all packed into the van. Connan claimed the front seat as he was the oldest. No one could argue that point. It also stopped Dean and Tracy from fighting over it. He had his ball cap on so that he wouldn't see Tracy glaring at him for taking her spot. Tracy sat between James and Troy in the seat behind them and Dean and Derek took the back row of seats.

Troy's doctor's appointment went well, considering his past of being born addicted to opioids. His speech was behind along with his growth, but he had improved since his last visit. Grace pulled into the mall parking lot and started addressing her kids.

"Tracy, you, Dean, and Derek can go to the arcade. James can go too if he behaves himself. Troy comes with me and so do you." She looked at Connan as she put the van in park. "You are not to leave my side."

"Yes, ma'am." Connan rolled his eyes but didn't argue. He needed those shoes if he was going to continue to coach Tracy for track. Her tryouts were only a couple weeks away. Connan told Grace exactly where he needed to go and they split with the others at the arcade. Connan placed his hat on backwards as he tried on tennis shoes. Out of the corner of his eye, he saw a mall cop talking to Grace. He didn't think much of it as Grace liked to talk to people. He finally found a good pair of running shoes, paid for them, and went back out to her.

"I got what I needed, Mom, these should last a bit longer than the last pair." He looked up at the tall mall cop. His eyes grew wide. He froze.

"Razor?" Concern etched Grace's face. "Razor? Are you alright?"

Connan took control of himself. "Yeah, sorry, zoned out for a sec. Is it okay if I talk to the cop alone for a sec?" He leaned and whispered in Grace's ear. "I'd like to apologize for causing a scene. He was on duty and told me to leave after I hit Frank."

"Sure, honey, we'll head to the arcade. I'm sure your dad wouldn't mind." Grace turned to leave. "Nice to meet you, Mr. Moore."

"Please, call me Randy." Connan froze as the familiar voice flowed from the man. "It was nice to meet you as well."

Connan stood frozen for a few minutes. "Snap out of it before you make a scene," Daryn hissed. He led him over to a secluded hall that had a sign at the entrance that said *Staff Only.* "Where is he?"

Connan couldn't speak. Fear accented his features. He shook his head. Daryn looked around. "Come on! Connan, I don't want to hurt you, but if you don't give him up, I'll have to!" Daryn pushed him against the wall. "I'd hate for you to have to take the fall for your dad, so tell me where he is!"

"I . . . I don't know where he is. I gave the burner phone to her husband. I have no contact with him. Please, just leave me out of this!" Connan tried to shake Daryn off but his grip was hard as steel. "I'm finally happy. I'm where I belong! Just let me go! Find Dad, do what you have to, but leave me out of it! I don't want to go back there! I'd rather die than go back to Denver!"

Daryn looked back toward the mall to see if any were watching the exchange. "Look, my boss wants Hyatt blood and if I can't find your dad, then you will have to take his place . . . Connan, I don't want to kill you. Just tell me where he is."

"I told you, I don't know! Pretend you didn't find me!" Connan tried to get loose again.

"I can't do that, and you know it. I've been trying to track Todd, but he's vanished. If I have to use you to get to him, I will. Don't make me do that . . . Who's the woman with the child?" Daryn got in his face. "You are making this very hard, Connan. Are they your cover? Is she a witness protection agent?"

"I had no help from Dad!" Connan began to panic. "She's a cop's wife. I laid my bike down and her husband was called to the scene. They took me in, since Johnny gave me the cover of a foster kid. They don't know anything! Please leave them out of this!"

"I knew Johnny was involved! I will do whatever it takes." Daryn released him. "Get me your dad or I'll have no choice but to hurt that family . . . and you."

Connan nodded ever so slightly and Daryn motioned for him to get lost. Connan walked as quickly as he dared to the arcade. He tried to act as if everything was okay once he rejoined Grace.

"Where is the officer?" Grace scanned the mall.

"He was called to a store. Someone was trying to steal stuff." Connan didn't dare tell her what had happened.

"Razor, are you alright, you look pale. You're shaking."

Connan looked over his shoulder, scanning the mall. "I don't feel all that good. If the others don't care, I'd like to go home."

Grace felt his forehead. "We'll go home."

13

DEREK TUGGED ON Grace's shirt. "What is it, Derek?" He pointed at Connan then looked up at her. She could see the concern in the thirteen-year-old's eyes. "He's not been right since the mall," Grace whispered. "He's been really fidgety . . . I'll talk to Dad about it. Razor won't talk to me right now and if he thinks I'm snooping, he will stop talking all together."

Derek pointed at himself then walked to the living room where Connan sat. Derek pulled at him. "Huh?" Connan jumped. "Derek, I'm really not in the mood. Sorry, buddy." Connan checked the clock again. *Come on, Cap, I need you! I need that phone! I'm running out of time!* Derek finally succeeded in pulling him up the stairs to show him the progress he was making on his computer build.

"Dad's home!" Dean said as he walked in the house from taking care of the animals.

"Alright, everyone, clear out. I need to talk to your dad alone." Grace shewed everyone up the stairs.

John walked in the door. "What a day!" He bent over and started unlacing his boots. "Where is everybody?" He kicked his shoes off then went and kissed his wife.

"I made them go upstairs." Grace wrapped her arms around his neck.

"Oh? And why would you put all our kids on the same floor at the same time?" John winked at her.

Grace remained serious. "Something happened to Connan . . . He won't speak . . . He jumps at every little thing . . . John, something happened at the mall that he's not telling me. He looks really scared. I think it may have to do with the mall officer. He wanted a moment alone with the gentlemen to apologize for his actions against Frank, then he's suddenly pale and sweating and acting all nervous!"

John let go of her. "I'll take care of it." He went to the stairs and called him down. "Razor! I need to talk to you! Get down here!"

John hadn't even finished unlocking his office when Connan charged down the stairs. "I need to talk to you, Cap!"

"In here, away from little ears." John opened the door and made Connan sit down in front of his desk.

John could see right away what Grace had been talking about. Connan's knee bounced up and down. His eyes kept darting to the windows. John closed the door and locked them in. "What's going on? You are acting very nervous and don't lie to me." John took his seat behind the desk.

It took Connan a few minutes to speak. "I . . . I ran into Daryn at the mall . . . He knows I'm here." Connan began to shake. "He saw me with Grace and Troy. He said he'd hurt them if I didn't tell him where dad is . . ."

"Did you tell Grace?"

"No, I didn't want her to worry."

"Was he disguised?"

"He was going by the name Randy Moore. A mall cop, his hair is darker than before . . . He could've taken me, right there. He said he didn't want to kill me but if he couldn't find my dad his boss would have him kill me. He wants Hyatt blood, whether it's mine or Dad's."

"Connan, calm down. With this, I can call it in and they will be able to arrest him if he's still there."

"He won't be there!" Connan got up and started to pace back and forth across the room. "He found me, that's all he needed to do. He had to find me and threaten me and those around me to get what he wants. He won't reappear till he comes for the information he wanted. He said he'd leave me out of it if I just told him where Dad was." Connan stopped pacing and sat back down. "I need to leave . . . He's found me, he's seen who I was with and even talked to Grace. The only way to keep them safe is for me to leave or for you to put me in lockup."

"You are not going anywhere." John was dialing a number. "Just hold tight, we will figure this out." He called in a favor and four police officers showed up for dinner. After James and Troy were put to bed, he gathered the rest of the family.

"Razor has been with us for a couple of months now . . . This may come as a shock to you, but his real name is Connan Hyatt. He's the kid that was plastered all over the news as an endangered teen. Dean knows his real name because I let it slip when he took off." John stopped and looked at Tracy. "I think you know too."

"Yes. He told me after we fought . . . He wanted me to understand why I hurt him so bad." Tracy lowered her head.

John continued. "The man who is after him found him this afternoon at the mall." Everyone looked up at him wide-eyed.

"But how did he find him?" Grace asked. "He's been so careful!"

"It only took one irrational thought." John looked at Connan then pulled up a video tube clip. "This is how he found him. I just discovered this myself." It was a clip of Connan and Frank. Tracy cheered along with Dean as Connan sent Frank to the floor. "Someone caught this on camera, and I'm convinced it's how they found him. The man who is after him was disguised as a mall cop."

Grace put a hand to her mouth. "Connan, you told me he was on duty when you hit Frank and you wanted to apologize."

"I . . ." Connan looked from her to John then back. "I didn't want you to get hurt . . . I got him alone, so he wouldn't hurt you or even attempt to."

"It doesn't matter now. All that matters is that you stay alert. You have all been warned. We weren't able to track him down at the mall, so he is still MIA." John took a deep breath before continuing. "The man chasing Connan has not only threatened him but has also said if Connan doesn't deliver he will come after this family." Everyone sat deathly still.

"We can't let them have him!" Dean said. "He's OUR brother now. They can't have him! What can we do?" His eyes watered.

"Connan will stay here, and we will keep a shift of officers on duty here. He's not to be left alone again. All of us need to be watchful and keep our eyes peeled for this man." John pulled up a picture of Daryn and a recent photo from the mall.

"His hair is darker now and not red like this photo shows. Be careful. We can't take any unnecessary risks. We're going to make it look as if Connan skipped town. I will also be getting a hold of Todd Hyatt and inform him that his son is in danger." John turned the TV off. "Everyone knows now, and you are all to use his fake name, got it?"

Everyone nodded their heads. John dismissed the family and set up the security measures. Connan couldn't stop his fear from growing. Bailey was once again at his side constantly. It comforted him a little knowing he had the dog by his side. John would take his shifts from home and take his turns on patrol around the house.

John sat in his office with Connan leaning over the other side of the desk. "I think it best you call him, then I'll explain what's going on." John handed Connan his burner phone. Connan dialed his dad's number and placed the phone on speaker.

"Connan?" Todd's voice came and went as if the call kept dropping. "You shouldn't be calling . . . Daryn could find you!"

"Dad, he . . ." Todd cut him off.

"Son, I have really bad signal, stay safe." The phone went silent.

"He never listens!" Connan blew up in his frustration. "I've always had to fight for his attention and that always ended with me in a county lockup! All he cares about is his own life!"

"Connan! You need to calm down and think." John pointed down as if to say "Sit down."

"I'm sorry . . . He always does this!" Connan sat down. "He's always unreliable when I need him most."

"We can try again tomorrow." John took the phone back. "We won't stop till we get through to him. Good news is, this has hit the news; so, hopefully, Daryn skips town and decides to leave you out of it."

"I doubt it." Connan tried to remain calm. "He seems desperate. He really doesn't want to hurt me, but by the sound of it his boss doesn't care about anything but Hyatt blood being spilled . . . He will be in contact one way or another . . . Too bad he didn't just go for Mom. No one likes her anyway."

"Is your dad's phone traceable?" John ignored his last sentence.

"No. He keeps it off for the most part and keeps his calls too short to be tracked."

"He covers his steps. I'll send a message through the phone and also try calling from the home phone."

"That's his job . . . He can make anyone disappear then shows up in time for court." Connan got up. "If I sit here any longer, I'll go crazy. I'm going to go see if Derek needs any help on his computer."

John nodded and Connan left the room. He ran back up to the twin's room and found Derek connecting the last pieces. "Looking good, bud!" He looked over the machine and found no errors. They took it down and plugged it into the TV to make sure it worked correctly. Connan showed him how to install a firewall then they downloaded a zombie game and connected controllers. Dean soon joined them.

John sat in his office and dialed Todd's number. *Voice mail again . . . He's turned his phone off . . . I can't even imagine cutting my kids off like this! Does he even care that his son is in danger?*

14

THE RIGBY HOUSEHOLD was under high alert for the next two weeks. Tracy's track tryouts were coming up. She kept begging John to let Connan come, but he refused.

"We have to keep him safe. If he goes, this Daryn guy could take him. We aren't taking that chance." John put his work belt on. "I have to go to the office tonight and won't be back till tomorrow evening but I've asked Meg to put me out of service during your track tryouts. You can tell Connan all about the tryouts once you get home."

"It's not the same!" Tracy tried again.

"Just drop it, sis." Connan walked into the kitchen. "I need to stay. I want to go, but I don't want to put you or any of the others in danger. It's safer if I stay home . . . Besides, Dean and Derek are staying with me, so I won't be alone." He leaned on the island countertop. "Plus, telling me all about how you got on the team and had the best time will be awesome!" He smiled at her.

"See, he agrees." John walked to the door where Grace was waiting. "I'll see you at the tryouts." He kissed her and disappeared out the door.

The Rigby house was louder than usual that night. Connan, Dean, and Derek went on a cheering spree every time Tracy would walk through the living room. Grace made homemade pizza for dinner and they all took turns playing a game on the console the boys brought down from their room. Grace even played a few rounds. The three oldest boys stayed up later in the night than the rest of them since they didn't have to be up early. They camped out in the living room playing games and telling scary stories. Dean and Connan did all the talking while Derek did a lot of grinning.

Connan woke up early the next morning as Grace walked down the stairs with Troy in her arms and James following behind her. Connan wormed his way out from between the twins and gave her a hug. "Can you record Tracy's run for me?" He whispered. "I really want to see it!"

"I will see what I can do," Grace replied.

"Thanks, Mom." Connan gave her another hug then went to the restroom. When he came out Tracy was putting her shoes on at the dining room table.

"I'm glad you're up!" She whispered. "Thank you for training me, Connan . . . I don't think I would be this fast if I hadn't been trying to keep up with you all summer!"

"Knock 'em dead, sis." Connan whispered back and gave her a hug. "Mom said she'd try and record it, so I can watch it when you get back!"

"I'll do my best!" Tracy gave him a big smile and went to the door. "Ready, Mom?"

Connan watched as the van pulled out of the drive. He woke the twins and they went upstairs to get dressed. Connan dressed and met them outside to take care of the animals. The four cops on duty followed them as they did chores then asked them to go back in the house as soon as they were done. No one fussed. Connan called Bailey into the house with them. *I feel a lot better when he's close.*

They set up to continue their gaming marathon. Connan grabbed a plate of toast while the boys battled each other. He couldn't help but laugh at their fighting styles. Dean pressed all the buttons while Derek did combos of all sorts of moves. Bailey grabbed Connan's attention as his head whipped up. His ears were forward. The donkey had started braying.

"Hey, pause your game." Connan put down his plate and watched as Bailey went to the window and started growling. His ears began to lay back. Connan heard it too. A soft thud hit the side of the house. "Back door now!" Connan hissed. "Stay low! Bailey, come on! Lead the way!"

Connan had just opened the back door when he heard the front door crash open. "Go!" he hissed again. Bailey started growling as he trotted outside. Connan closed the back door as silently as he could then turned around. Three men who were definitely not cops had cut off any escape. An officer lay unmoving not far from the door. "Bailey, attack!"

Connan charged the one in the middle. Bailey charged the one on the right. "Run!" Connan yelled as he hit the one in the middle.

Derek and Dean lunged forward. Derek dodged both Connan and Bailey. The third man went to help fight Connan off. Connan hit the man with an upper cut sending him sprawling to the ground. The other he had knocked out cold. He took over for Bailey and Bailey pursued Derek to the wood line. Dean had stopped to examine one of the downed cops and tried to wake him.

"Dean! NO!" Connan ran toward him. Dean looked over his shoulder to see a tall man pointing a gun at him. As the man pulled the trigger, Connan dove in front of Dean. An electric charge coursed through his body, making his muscles seize. He bit his tongue as his jaws clamped shut.

"Razor!" Dean screamed as Connan fell to the ground in front of him. The man Connan had stunned picked Dean up off the ground. He started to fight, but the man was too strong for him.

The tall man stepped over Connan as he put a new cartridge in his Taser. "Take the kid with us. We may need him to make this one more cooperative." He tapped the Taser against Dean's chest. "You behave and I won't hurt your brother."

Dean stopped trying to free himself. He looked at Connan who had stopped moving. Blood poured from his mouth. The tall man bent down as he pulled out a pair of zip tie cuffs. Dean was dragged off around the house and Daryn started to tie Connan's hands behind his back. Connan could hardly do anything to defend himself as Daryn placed a knee on his back. "I didn't want to do this, Connan . . . You forced my hand."

Connan tried to fight off the men that pulled him up but stopped as soon as he saw Dean had not gotten away. "No, no, no, no!" Connan was marched to one of the two vehicles. Dean was placed into the other. "No! Daryn, let him go! Please!"

"Behave and I'll consider it." Daryn got into the front seat of the car as two of his men forced Connan into the back seat. "Let's get out of here, before the entire police department shows up. The other kid got away, so I'm sure he will be making a call soon."

The two vehicles spun gravel as they drove off in the opposite direction of town. Daryn took a syringe from a box and turned toward Connan. Can't have you trying to wreck us now, can I? He stabbed it into Connan's leg and injected the anesthetic. Connan tried to fight it, but it was too strong.

Meanwhile, Derek and Bailey cautiously returned to the house. He checked to see if the officers were alive. He jumped back as one of the officers stirred. Bailey licked the man's face.

The man sat up suddenly. He got to his feet and took out his radio. "Dispatch, this is Officer Carter stationed at the Rigby home. We've been attacked. All officers down, only one of the kids are accounted for." He moved to the front of the house. "Attackers are gone, left a note for Captain Rigby and a phone. We need an ambulance!"

Ten minutes later Captain Rigby drifted into the drive. Three of the officers were on their feet and a medic crew was loading the fourth into an ambulance. Carter met Rigby as he jumped out of his car.

"Dean and Connan were taken. Derek was able to wake me up." They walked to the porch. "They came from the woods and hit us with gas pellets. Tripp was the only one they shot. They left these." Officer Carter handed him the phone and the note.

"You have twelve hours to bring me Todd Hyatt or I will kill Connan." John wadded the note up. I have a call to make. Derek followed him inside. He pulled on his dad's belt and motioned for him to follow.

Derek started to set up his computer. "Phone, Dad, I need the number and the phone Connan used before."

Stunned that he had heard Derek speak for the first time, he ran to his office. He grabbed the phone and ran back to the living room. Derek connected it to his computer and dialed the number. An older version of Connan appeared on the TV screen.

"Connan, you have to stop calling me and how on earth were you able to video chat me?" Derek held the phone up and turned the camera so that Todd could see John. Todd's attitude changed. "Who are you? Where is my son?"

"We don't have time for pleasantries." John resisted the urge to start pacing. "My name is John Rigby, Captain at the New Crosley Police Department in Indiana. Daryn Moroe has found your son."

"How do I know you're telling the truth?" Todd questioned. "I need proof if I am to believe you."

"We don't have time for this! Connan has been staying with me under cover as one of my foster children. We don't have time to discuss all of this! He's been taken by Daryn and you have less than twelve hours to save him. Daryn is going to take his life if he can't have you." John looked at the man on the screen. "You better burn rubber because he's not the only one Daryn took. He took my thirteen-year-old too. We've been trying to get a hold of you for two weeks!"

Todd avoided John's fiery eyes. "I . . . I won't make it in time . . . I am hiding outside of the country . . . I flew commercially and don't have access to my jet . . . I can't help you."

"Coward! You leave your son to fend for himself while you flee to save your own skin! You've condemned him to death!" John took a deep breath to calm his anger. "You better believe that I will be taking you to court for custody if I get him out of YOUR mess alive!" John ran a hand across his throat and Derek disconnected the call. He pulled Derek into a hug. "We've got to save them . . . Hyatt is no help!" John released Derek and walked toward the door. "Get your shoes on, Derek. We're calling a meeting at the station with the Operations Captain and the chief!"

Derek hurried to put his shoes on and ran to his dad's car. He jumped in while John told Officer Carter his plan. "Go to the high school and escort my family to the station. Hopefully, Tracy has already ran. It's about time we take care of this ourselves. We can save them, and we'll have God and the department at our backs!"

15

CONNAN BEGAN TO wake. He shook his head. "Connan? You awake?" Dean was pushing on his back. Connan tried to turn to see him. "They tied us back-to-back. Are you okay?" Dean sniffed as if he'd been crying.

"I'm fine," Connan replied. "Where are we?" The taste of blood in his mouth made his stomach sick. "Are you? Did he hurt you?" His tongue was a little swollen and made it hard to speak.

"No... Connan, I'm scared." Dean squirmed. "I'm sorry. This is all my fault! If I hadn't tried to wake Carter, we would've gotten away!"

"Calm down," Connan said as he pushed on Dean. "We'll think of something . . . We have to. What time is it?"

"I don't know but it looks like the sun is going down. Too bad they tied us up, I could probably fit through the window!"

Connan shook his head again. "They probably sealed it off or have someone outside the window to make sure that doesn't happen . . . Daryn is smart so don't do anything stupid, okay? He's dangerous."

Dean leaned his head back onto Connan's shoulder. "I'm scared, Connan. What if he . . . ?"

"I won't let him hurt you." Connan cut in. "As long as we don't fight him, he won't hurt you."

"He could hurt you . . . I don't want him to hurt you!"

"I'll be fine. Just try to stay calm okay, buddy? Dad will come."

The door opened and two men came in. They cut the rope that tied the two boys together. One picked Dean up off the floor and the other pulled Connan to his feet. He was clumsy from the drugs they had injected and his muscles didn't want to work. They half dragged him out of the room. They pushed Connan into a chair and kept Dean away from him but where he could see him. Daryn stepped in front of him.

"Your dear old dad has less than twelve hours to show up, or I'll have to take your life." Daryn lifted Connan's chin to make him look at him. "I didn't want to involve you, kid, but you involved the police again and I couldn't get to you. I'm sorry it's come to this . . . Your dad should've known I'd find you." Daryn nodded at the man holding Dean and the man brought him to him. Daryn stepped away from Connan to take hold of Dean.

"Please! Don't hurt him!" Connan tried to stand but strong arms kept him seated. "Just let him go! He has nothing to do with this! I'll do anything, just don't hurt him!"

"Connan, you forced my hand." Daryn forced Dean to his knees and put a gun to his head. Dean started to cry.

"No! Please!" Connan slid down to avoid the men behind him. He stood up. "You kill him, and you'll have to kill me! I will fight till I die! Let him go!" The two men took hold of Connan.

"Leave him." Daryn cocked the hammer back on his revolver. "Let's see just how well you do as your told." He directed his men to cut Connan loose. "Now you are going to sit back down and stay there. If you don't. I'll kill him." He pressed the gun barrel hard against Dean's head, making him cry out.

Connan felt the ties slip off. He looked at Dean who had tears rolling down his cheeks. "Dean, look at me!" Connan backed up to the chair. "It's okay, bud, just look at me." Connan sat down and leaned back. "Now, let him go."

"In a minute . . . I have a call to make first." Daryn took a cell phone out of his pocket and dialed a number. "Captain. The name's Daryn Moroe. Have you heard from Mr. Hyatt . . . ?" Daryn looked up and Connan with a sad expression on his face. "Well, that's a crying shame . . . Well, here's the deal, Captain . . ." Daryn walked away and started talking in a whisper. Connan went to get up but saw Daryn watching him. He talked a few minutes longer then hung up the phone and went back to Dean. He pulled him back up and handed him over to one of his men.

"Where are you taking him?" Connan stood up. "Tell me!"

"Sit down!" Daryn started pacing.

"What? Daryn? Talk to me! Don't hide it from me, what did Cap say?" Connan tried to calm his nerves.

"I didn't want to do this, Connan . . ." Daryn stopped and looked at him. "I thought for sure your dad would protect you at any cost!"

Connan felt as if the wind had been knocked out of him. He sat down. "He's not coming, is he? He always seems to disappear or show up too late when I need him most, doesn't he? Typical." Connan went deathly calm. He stopped shaking. "Do me a favor, would you?"

"What's that?" Daryn took a couple steps forward as if concerned for Connan.

"Don't let Dean see you do it . . ." Connan stared at the floor. "Don't let him see you shoot me. I would gladly take a bullet right now, but I want to talk to him . . . alone."

"What, no fighting? No foul language?"

"I'd rather be dead," Connan kept his eyes on the floor, stone-faced. "He's not coming. I have no family. I'm taking the fall for good this time."

"I'm sorry, Connan . . . I . . . I'll let you talk to the kid."

"The only thing I care about now is in this building." Connan got up and met Daryn in the middle of the room. "And I want you to let him go . . . I don't have a family, but he does. Don't take him from them." Two men secured Connan and marched him away.

Daryn stared after him as if he should've fought for his life more. "Poor kid . . . Take the younger one to the same room at nine. Give them an hour alone, then bring Connan to me. Boss wants it on video before eleven."

Connan sat on the floor against the back wall of the empty office. *Again, he leaves me to fend for myself . . . He's never really loved me, has he? If he did, he'd drop everything like Cap did when I walked off that day . . . If there is a god up there . . . Can you hear me? Would you listen to me? I really just want to die now! Just take my life now! I'm nothing but an empty shell!* Connan roared in his thoughts. *If you are there, then just kill me now! Please! I don't want to live!* He leaned forward, resting his head on his forearms. *I've got no one . . . what is so wrong with me that they would leave me?*

Connan had no tears. He sat almost as still as a statue for the next few hours. The door opened and a man brought Dean in. "Boss says you have an hour, then you have to come with me."

Connan stood, still blank-faced. "Understood." The man left, closing the door behind him. Connan rushed over and untied Dean.

"I was so scared! Connan, he was going to kill me!" Dean cried into Connan's shoulder.

"He won't hurt you as long as I do what he wants." Connan hugged him tight. "Whatever happens, I want you to know that you are the best brother I could ever have . . . Tell your dad, thanks for taking me in . . . and Grace, tell her she's the best mom I ever had. They gave me a different view of what the world could look like."

Dean started to panic. "No! Dad will come! He'll save us!"

"Dean, he has an hour . . . an hour to find us and stop Daryn from putting a bullet in . . ." Connan pulled him away so he could look him in the eyes. "Dean, he's going to kill me . . . When that door opens, I will go with that man, and I won't be coming back."

Dean shook his head. "You can't! Connan, you can't go! I won't let you!"

"If I don't, he will kill you too." Connan looked at the door still deathly calm. "If I go out that door willingly, you will live."

"I don't want you to die!"

Connan sat down. "My life is all I have left. I'm just an empty shell now, but if I can save you . . . Do you think Jesus would spare me from hell? I read something about saving your life will lose it but losing your life will save it . . . Does that mean if I die to keep you safe, it would save me from hell?"

"I don't think it works like that!" Dean sat down in front of Connan. "You have to have Jesus in your heart . . . Do you know Him?"

Connan shook his head and looked away. "I've never heard the name as a good thing till I started reading Cap's book before anyone got up. I've never heard his name other than when someone's cussing. Cap had told me a story and said it came from the Bible, so I decided to find it. I've been trying to read every morning he's on shift."

"Dad could explain it to you when we get out of here." Dean started looking around the room. "We have to do something to get both of us out."

"Dean, I'm not walking out. I don't think I even want to. The only way you are walking out of here is if I walk through that door."

"I said both of us! Your dad isn't coming but mine is!" Dean lowered his voice. "He's got an entire police department to back him up! He's not going to let them kill us! Don't give up!"

"Dean, he has less than an hour to find us." Connan remained deathly calm. "I just don't see any hope of rescue for me . . . I'm already dead."

"Don't talk like that! We have to do something!" Dean stood up. "We could rush the door when they come for you!"

Connan shook his head. "There are two guys outside the door, we'd be caught immediately, and he'd make you watch me die or he'd make me watch you die . . . I can't let that happen, Dean. I have to protect you at all costs!" Connan stayed rooted to the spot. "I won't let you die."

"The door opens inward . . . maybe we could keep them out?"

"Two teens against half a dozen armed adults . . . that would go over well."

"Got a better idea that doesn't get you killed?"

Connan shook his head. "No, it's the only thing I can do to keep you safe."

Dean crossed his arms. "I'm not letting you do it! I won't! You may have given up hope for us both to get out, but I haven't! God will get us out!"

"I'm useless to God, why would He want me? He never answers me . . . No, you are getting out of here. I'm dying here."

"Stop!" Dean grabbed Connan's shirt and tried to shake him. Tears streamed down his face. "Stop acting like you are already dead! I won't let you die! You hear me! I won't let you die!"

"It's too late, Dean . . . It's too late." Tears silently rolled down his face. "I'm dead already, nothing can change that."

It seemed as if only a few minutes had passed when the door started to open. Dean lunged for it and rammed his shoulder into it. "You can't have him! I won't let him die!"

"Now you've done it!" Connan stood. "Why, Dean? Now he's gonna kill both of us!"

"I'd rather die with you than separate from you! You really think he's not going to kill me? He's not exactly a promise keeper by what I've heard. God, get us out of here alive!" Dean shouted as loud as he could.

"Never thought of it that way . . ." Connan waited for the door to open slightly. Someone's arm appeared between the door and its frame. "Move, Dean!" Connan kicked the door as hard as he could. A scream issued from the other side and the arm disappeared again. Dean launched himself against the door again.

Connan braced himself against it too. A knock sounded from the other side. "Wrong move, kid . . . Come out now and I'll keep my word."

"No, you won't!" Dean yelled. "I won't let him die! He's my brother, not your plaything!"

"Connan, I'll kill him! Come out, now!" Daryn was enraged.

"He's right, you know!" Connan shouted back. "How do I know you won't just kill him after you off me? Your word doesn't mean much to me since you betrayed me!"

"I never betrayed you! I am getting paid to kill a Hyatt and I was after your dad! Should've kept your nose out of it! You shouldn't have posted that video!"

"You never cared about me, did you? You only wanted free room and board and the money, didn't you?" Someone slammed into the door, but Connan and Dean held their position.

"Some days you were just as annoying as you're being right now, but other days I thought you an okay kid." Daryn knocked into the door himself. "If I have to come in after you, I'll kill the kid with no hesitation!"

"Okay, okay, you win! I'll come out . . ." He braced himself against the door. "When I'm good and ready. I need more time with Dean!"

"Break it down! Bring them both to the bay!" Daryn's voice faded as he walked away.

"We can hold them off! I know we can!" Dean pushed as hard as he could. "Dad, please hurry!"

16

"YOU HAVE YOUR orders, roll out!" Captain Rigby rode in the front passenger seat of the SWAT truck. *Lord, don't let us be too late! Those boys need you more than they know! Protect them, Jesus. Let us be on time!*

The truck pulled out of the police department. They kept their lights and sirens off so they wouldn't alert any guards that may be placed. They had thirty minutes left of the twelve hours. They had to be on time. They parked far enough away from the old warehouse where Daryn's phone had been traced.

The team split into groups to surround the building.

"No heat signatures outside the building. Nine detected inside." A sniper called over the radio. "Looks like the kids are fighting for more time. Four men are pushing against the boys. Looks like they are trying to keep them out of a room."

"Do you have eyes on Daryn Moroe?" John relayed back.

"We have eyes on Moroe. He's in the bay with two others. The boys are really giving these men a run for their money. Two of them are about to kick in the door."

"All in position?" John asked over the radio as he crouched beside a door near the bay entrance.

"In position," came the reply.

"On my mark," Rigby whispered.

* * *

Connan and Dean pressed themselves against the door. Dean was shaking from the exertion. "I'm getting tired, Connan. I don't think I can do this much longer."

"Me too, bud." Connan began to whisper. "If we move away, they will crash through on their next attempt, and we could possibly make a break for it or at least fight our way past." *He has to reach the door. Daryn can kill me, but I won't let him kill Dean. I'll force him to keep his word . . . Even if I have to fight him for a time.*

"Okay." Dean pushed as the men hit the door again.

"Here," Connan whispered. "Get to the side." He pushed Dean over, so he wasn't behind the door. "If we let them run in maybe we can lock them in if all four come through."

They crouched and waited for the men to hit the door again. CRASH! Two of the men fell as they kicked the door open with no resistance. Connan and Dean dashed out the door catching the other two off guard. The two men with Daryn launched themselves across the bay when they saw the escapees.

"Don't let them get to the door!" Daryn yelled. He ran at Connan while the other two ran at Dean.

The first reached Dean but Connan plowed into him. He went for a low tackle as the man was smaller. Daryn caught up and seized the back of Connan's shirt. "Get the brat!" Daryn yelled as he pulled Connan to the ground. Connan tried to fight him off, but he wasn't strong enough. Daryn punched him hard across the jaw, making him see stars.

Daryn pulled him up and half dragged him to a part of the bay that had been covered with plastic sheets. "Nice try, but you'll have to do better than that." He forced Connan to his knees and pressed a gun to his head. Dean was pushed down to his knees in front of Connan. The man behind him was holding him by the hair.

"I was going to let you go." He addressed Dean. "I will still let you go as a favor to Connan, but now you have to watch him die!" Daryn cocked the hammer back.

"Close your eyes." Connan tried to get away, but Daryn kept a firm hold on him with his other hand. "Dean, close your eyes." He calmed himself, ready to take the bullet meant for his dad. *God, why didn't you let Dean get away?* "I'm sorry, Dean. I didn't want you to see this!" He closed his eyes and took a deep breath expecting it to be his last.

"NO!" Dean cried. "NO!"

BANG! Connan didn't dare open his eyes. *God, I don't want to go to hell!* Someone pulled him down to the ground. Gunfire broke out around him, but he kept his eyes closed.

"Connan! Wake up!" A familiar voice rang in his ears. "Get the medics in here! Dean, are you okay?"

"I'm fine, Dad! Connan, Dad came! He came! You're not dead!" Dean tried to shake him awake. "You're okay, Connan! Snap out of it!"

Connan didn't understand. Was he dead? The voices around him were muffled. Blood had splattered all over him. He started shaking. He slowly opened his eyes as the medics lifted him onto a stretcher. A blanket was placed over him. "He's in shock." Connan heard the medic talking as they loaded him into the ambulance. "Were going to have to sedate him to calm him down."

"I'm going with him!" Dean jumped in the passenger seat of the ambulance. "I want to be there if he comes out of it!"

John nodded and turned back to the scene. He dialed Grace's number. "We got them . . . They are both alive, but Connan is in terrible shock. Daryn was about to kill him when we opened fire . . . He was the first to go down. He had his gun to Connan's head when we took him . . . Dean is a strong boy, he's riding in the ambulance that just left with Connan .

. . You remember what you told me before? I want you to call Eldree . . . I love you too, bye."

Connan found himself in a hospital room when he woke up. He bolted upright.

"Take it easy, son." John sat in a chair next to his bed.

"Where's Dean? Is he okay? Did he make it out? Daryn said he was letting him go!" Connan started to shake again. "Am . . . Am I dead?"

"Calm down, Connan." John scooted closer. "He's fine, you're fine, and Daryn can't hurt you ever again."

"He . . . He never came." Connan tried to hold back the tears. It made him shake even worse than before. "Dad didn't come! He was going to let me die!" He balled his hands into fists as he tried hard not to cry. The monitors started to beep rather loudly.

A doctor rushed into the room as John tried to lay Connan back down. Connan swung wildly at him. "He's unstable at best." The doctor said. "I'm going to give him something to calm down."

"Do it." John said as he pinned Connan's arms. "Connan, stop! No one can hurt you!"

"Just let me die!" Connan tried to fight John off. "I don't want to live! Let go!"

Once a dose of Valium had been administered the doctor had him restrained. "This is for our safety as much as it is yours." The doctor took John aside. "He could possibly develop PTSD if he doesn't see a psychiatrist. I'd recommend him seeing our in-house psychiatrist, Doctor Long. I also would like Doctor Long to monitor him for a few days. He's too unstable to go home at this point."

"I understand. I think he should see Dean if you think it possible." John looked at the doctor. "It may help him."

"Not till he can stay calm without medication . . . He needs to rest and be away from everything. I'm going to have him moved to an isolated room where it will be quiet." The doctor picked up Connan's chart and copied vitals down on it. "I'll inform you once he's stable enough to be moved."

John nodded and looked back at Connan. He still shook and his eyes were tightly closed. "I have some work to do. You have my number if anything changes." He left the room and headed for the waiting room where the rest of his family sat.

"Is he okay?" Dean asked with a shaky voice.

"I pray he will be. Right now, he needs rest. I don't know why he's reacted the way he has to this, but pray he snaps out of it."

"What did the doctor say?" Grace stood up and picked up Troy. "Let's get going. If he needs rest, we won't be able to see him for a while."

"Grace," John pulled her aside. "We had to restrain him . . . I don't know what happened in there, but whatever it was, he's not in a good place. He told us to let him die." John's eyes started to water. "Pray the Lord helps him. He's in a lot of pain right now mentally."

Grace hugged him. "You may see if Dean can help shed some light since he was with him." She kissed his cheek. "I think Dean can handle it. He wasn't affected like Connan was."

"I'll talk to him. If anything comes from it, I'll call the doctor . . . In the meantime, did you set up a meeting with Eldree?"

Grace nodded. She dug a slip of paper out of her purse. "He asked if you could meet him at the station once you're done here. He said he had business over there."

"I'll head over now." He stopped Dean as he walked out of the sitting room. "Hey, want to go with me down to the station?"

"Yeah, I'll go." Dean stepped aside while the others piled out of the room.

"Dean," John said as they got into his patrol car. "Can you tell me anything that might help us help Connan?"

"You want to know what happened?" Dean looked up at him. "It was real bad . . . ."

"I understand if you don't want to talk about it."

"No, I can tell you . . ." Dean took a deep breath then dove right in. "It's my fault we didn't get away like Derek. I tried to wake Carter up, but the tall guy snuck up behind me. Connan tried to protect me and got tased. He and Bailey had taken out three of the dudes, but the tall guy showed up out of nowhere. He was going to tase me, but Connan jumped in the way . . . One of his men grabbed me and he told him to take me along so Connan would cooperate." Dean paused. "He said that if I behaved he wouldn't hurt Connan, so I didn't fight back . . . I didn't want him to hurt him."

Dean's breathing became slightly heavier. "When we got to the warehouse, they dragged Connan out of the car. He wasn't awake. They tied us together in a small room and left us there. Once Connan was awake, they came back. The tall guy put a gun to my head and Connan freaked out . . . Said he'd do anything the guy wanted if he would let me go . . . The guy walked away and called you then came back and said that Connan's dad wasn't coming . . ." Dean sniffed. "They separated us, and I thought for sure he was going to kill Connan. After an hour or so, he gave us an hour to be together before he . . ." A tear ran down Dean's cheek. "Connan wasn't the same when I saw him again. It's like the light had been sucked out of him . . . He asked if Jesus would spare him from hell if he was able to save my life by dying willingly . . ." Dean's lip began to tremble. "Dad, he doesn't know Jesus . . . He just gave up."

"It's okay if you need to stop . . ." John's voice cracked. He was crying now too.

"It's okay, better get it out or I won't be able to later." Dean sniffed again and wiped his face. "I told him you would come for us, but he was already gone. When the men tried to open the door, I rammed into it and told them they couldn't have him . . . Connan was so surprised and hurt that I'd risk my life to try and save him. He eventually helped me, and we stayed against the door till we were too tired to keep them out. Connan had the idea to stand beside the door and run as they broke through the door. They crashed through and fell on top of each other. It surprised the other two outside, so we got away. Connan tackled one of the guys after me, but the tall guy got a hold of him and punched him really hard in the face. It was all over after that. I don't think Connan really wanted to get away . . . I think he was trying to make sure I got away . . . He wanted to die, Dad. Then all of a sudden he wanted to escape . . . I think he was trying to get me out then make sure they didn't follow."

Dean took another deep breath. "The other guy who had come after me grabbed me by the hair and carried me over to the plastic. Connan tried to get away, but the tall guy was too strong . . . He was going to kill him. He said he was still going to let me go but I had to watch Connan die . . ." Dean swallowed hard. "He had the gun to his head and Connan told me to close my eyes. He didn't want me seeing it happen . . . He wasn't even shaking! Then the tall guy and the guy holding me fell like potato sacks to the floor after a gun went off . . . You know the rest from there."

"I'll let the doctor know, they may be able to help him if they know what happened." John took a handkerchief out of his pocket and blew his nose. "He may have wished for his own death, but he could only think of saving you in the end."

"And I wouldn't let him . . . I hope he isn't mad at me . . . I didn't think the tall guy would let me go anyway. Figured he'd still kill me after killing Connan. I figured if we stalled them long enough you could save us . . . and you did!" Dean thought for a moment. "Do you think God would've spared Connan if he would've died? I mean, he doesn't know who Jesus is or at least he never did before he came. He told me he had been reading a bit from your Bible on the mornings you worked."

John finally put the car in gear. "I don't know, son . . . Did he really want to know if Jesus would spare him from hell if he was able to save you?"

"Yeah, I didn't really know what to tell him. I asked him if he knew Jesus and he told me he'd never known him as a good thing because he had only heard the name when someone was cussing."

"Another reason we're meeting Eldree . . . I thought he might be reading, since I've been finding marked corners . . . I never mark my corners." John pulled out of the hospital parking lot.

"Eldree?" Dean let the name sink in for a second. His eyes widened. "Yes!"

17

CONNAN DIDN'T IMPROVE. For the entire next week Connan fought the hospital staff. Two nurses had to go into his room together just to make sure he wouldn't try and run and so they could control him if he did try anything. Doctor Long didn't allow any female nurses in the room nor did he allow anything in the room that Connan could potentially kill himself with.

Grace paced the kitchen as she waited for John to get home one night. She had her shoes on and her purse sat on the counter. *Please, don't get held over! I need to see him!* Half an hour later the captain walked in.

"Hey," John said as he wrapped her into a hug. "You look worried, what's on your mind?"

"Connan," She replied. "I just . . . Don't laugh, but I have this feeling he needs me. John, I need to go see him, tonight."

John looked down at her. "I don't know if the doctor will let you see him . . . A couple of officers had to escort Mr. Hyatt out when he tried to see him last night. Doctor Long called me after and said Connan shouldn't be allowed near the man. Said he'd ask a judge for a restraining order with how Mr. Hyatt was acting."

"He was that rude to the doctors?"

"He was demanding that they release Connan right then and there so he could take him home. Doc told him he wasn't stable, and Todd told him he could handle Connan." John sighed. "Doctor Long made the right decision, but I think a restraining order would be too much. I invited Mr. Hyatt over to have a nice long talk." John looked down and noticed Grace was wearing her shoes. "I take it you are going to try to see Connan?"

Grace nodded, a determined look in her eyes. "I just have this feeling, John. I haven't been able to stop thinking about him all day.

It's almost as if he's on the brink of dying and I know I can help him. I have to go. I fear if I don't, he will die." She grabbed her purse off the counter. "Dinner is in the oven. Tracy is watching over it. She can entertain the boys while you have your talk with Mr. Hyatt. Don't let Dean know he's coming though . . . He's been fiery mad all week at the man for not even trying to save Connan."

"I'll make sure he's busy elsewhere." John kissed his wife. "Be safe on the road, and I'll see you when you get back."

Grace hugged her husband goodbye and left as quickly as she could. Worry engulfed her as she steered the van toward town. *Lord, I don't know what you're trying to tell me, but please don't let me be too late! He needs me!* She started praying aloud. "He's just a boy! His burden seems so heavy, and he doesn't know what love, or grace, or mercy is! Lord, don't let me be too late!"

She drove as quickly as she could and parked as close to the emergency entrance as possible. *It's a lot faster to go through there. Brenda will let me through, may even take me all the way up if I asked so I can bypass the security doors.* She calmed herself as she approached the doors. She greeted the receptionist.

"Brenda!"

"Grace Rigby!" the woman got up and ran around the desk to hug her friend. "We sure do miss you around here! Place hasn't been the same since you left! Your cousin still causes a bit of chaos when he's here!"

"I bet he does! It's great to see you, Brenda! Is there a chance you could help me get up to the psychiatric wing? I'm in a bit of a rush." Grace tried to be patient but the urgency in her mind kept trying to prod her forward. "It's urgent I get up there as fast as possible."

Brenda stared at her for a moment. "That's right! One of your boys was admitted!" She turned on her heel. "I'll walk you up!"

They moved as quickly as they could through the emergency room and out the other side to an elevator. Brenda took her all the way up to the third floor and used her badge to open the psychiatric ward. "I'll see you on the way back through if I'm not off by then!"

Grace said goodbye to her friend with a promise to meet for lunch sometime then made her way down to the nurse's desk. Doctor Long was standing at the counter.

"Doctor Long!" She greeted. "How is Connan? I've been so worried!"

"As well you should be, Mrs. Rigby." The doctor handed the nurse a chart before facing Grace. "He won't let anyone near him now. Started that behavior this morning. We can't even get close enough to administer medication. He won't eat, he refuses to communicate . . . Grace, I've had him on suicide watch for three days now. He's getting worse, not better."

"I knew something was wrong . . ." Grace looked around at the doors lining the hall. "Which room is he in?"

"Grace, he will hurt you if you go in there."

"I'll take my chances, Doctor Long." She stood defiant. "I will see him tonight. Not tomorrow, not next week, tonight. Any other time will be too late. He needs me . . . right now."

"Grace . . . ."

"Which room is he in, Doctor?" Her authoritative tone made Doctor Long take a step back.

"You can go in, ONLY," He put a finger up, "if a couple of nurses accompany you. I won't have you hurt on his account."

"Thank you, but I won't need them," Grace reassured him. "He won't hurt me."

"He's not the same, Grace." Doctor Long tried to persuade her once again. "He won't even let John near . . . He came by last night after Mr. Hyatt was escorted out."

"Connan won't hurt me," she insisted. "I am his mother, and he needs me! I will not take no for an answer Doctor Long and you know perfectly well that I will not let my boy suffer any longer."

Doctor Long gave a huge sigh then said, "I will stand at the door. If I think he's going to do anything to you, I will pull you out."

"That's acceptable." Grace gestured for him to lead the way.

Connan sat on the bed with his knees pulled up to his chest. He played with the drawstring on the scrubs he wore. He pulled on one end. *As long as they stay out I can end everything!* He pulled another inch or two out. *It will take some convincing to let me use the bathroom by myself . . . It only takes one good attempt . . . Then whatever is wrong with me will be gone for good.* He pulled the string another inch.

The door slid open, and Grace rushed into the room. Connan was so surprised he couldn't respond. She looked weary and afraid. Connan began to shake. *If I do this, I can't cause her anymore worry or harm.*

"Connan?" Grace slowly approached him. "Connan, please . . . May I sit with you?"

Connan couldn't respond. He wanted to yell at her and tell her to leave, but her demeanor kept him from speaking. She slowly sat down on the end of his bed. He couldn't hold back all of the emotion that started to swell within him. He pulled the string another inch. He began to tremble as Grace moved closer.

"Let me help you." Her soothing tone was calming. Tears started streaming down Connan's face. "Oh, honey." Grace was now sitting right beside him. She wrapped her arms around him as if he were no more than six years old. "Shh, it's okay; you're going to be just fine. I know you're hurting, but I'm right here. Shh, it's okay, baby; I'm here." She rocked back and forth as he melted into her arms.

Grace nodded at the doctor in a way that told Doctor Long to leave them alone. She rocked Connan as he cried bitter tears. He held onto her tightly as if she were the only light source in the world. She tried to contain her own tears, but they overflowed. She kissed the back of his head.

"Wha . . . what's . . . wrong . . . with me?" Connan stammered through the gasps of air. "Why . . . Why me?"

"There's nothing wrong with you . . ." Grace didn't even bother to wipe her tears away. "There is nothing wrong with you, honey." She kissed the back of his head again. "Some never learned how to love themselves so they can't give what they don't have. Connan, I love you so much! Nothing could ever change that! You are worth so much more than you know!"

Connan cried even harder and clung even tighter. *Please, don't be a dream! Please, don't be a dream!* They sat like this for some time. Crying and holding tight to one another. Finally, Connan relaxed his grip on her. He had fallen asleep. Grace gently laid him back on the bed. As she did, his waistband was exposed.

She gasped. *He was going to . . . Oh, God, You knew how to help him and You did!* She pulled the string completely out of the waistband then covered him with the blankets he had shoved to the bottom of the bed. She quietly got up and slid the door open. She stepped out the door. Doctor Long was waiting for her.

"How did you . . . ?"

"I told you, Doctor Long," she stated. "He needed his mother . . . He's sleeping now, I want you to bring up a recliner for me. I'm not leaving him alone." She held out her hand and showed him the drawstring. "He was inching this out of his waistband. He was going to try and kill himself on the next trip to the bathroom. I'm sure he would've succeeded too. I need to call John. Can I use your office?"

Doctor Long took the drawstring offered and nodded his head. Her words left him dumbfounded. "He was . . . I'll have a chair brought up right away."

Grace thanked him and he let her into his office at the end of the hall. There, she called her husband. "John? Have you met with Connan's dad . . . No, he was worse today than he was yesterday . . . John, he was going to hang himself, I know it. God knew what he was intending to do and sent me to him . . . He would've killed himself tonight, I'm sure of it . . . I need to stay with him. I had Doctor Long order a chair for me . . . He's sleeping right now. I don't want to be away for too long . . . Love you too, baby . . . Pray for him . . . love you, bye." Grace made her way back to Connan's room. A nurse let her back in. Connan was still sound asleep. He had curled into a fetal position.

A few minutes later, Grace's chair arrived. She had it placed as close to the bed as possible. All night, she watched Connan; if he started to shake, she'd take his hand in hers and console him with soothing words. Only in the early morning hours did she drift off to sleep.

Connan woke with a start. *Was that a dream?* He felt the soft, warm hand of Grace holding his. *She . . . That's the first time anyone has ever told me they loved me . . .* He looked at her as she lay asleep in the recliner. He started to tremble. *I've always been alone . . . alone and forgotten . . . but she loves me! A perfect stranger, but she still dropped everything to . . . to save me . . . I was going to kill myself and she shows up before I could . . . Somehow she knew and came!* Tears streamed down his cheeks once again. *She saved me . . . I can live for her . . . for her love.*

Connan gently let go of her hand and stumbled toward the bathroom. The lack of solid foods and not enough fluids was starting to take a toll on his body. *A shower should help.* He thought. *A long, hot one.*

Grace woke in a panic. "Connan!" Her heart began to race when she found he wasn't in the bed beside her.

"I'm here." Connan leaned out of the bathroom so Grace could see him. "Be out in a sec."

Grace put her hand on her chest. "Oh, thank goodness! For a second I thought you might have . . ." She picked up her phone. "What do you want for breakfast?"

Connan stepped out of the bathroom. "Pancakes? Blueberry pancakes with a side of bacon?" He held onto the wall to keep himself from falling.

"Connan!" Grace rushed over and put an arm around his waist. "Come, sit down."

"I'm just a little dizzy, I'll be okay." Connan let her help him without complaint. "Could I have some coffee too? With cream?"

Grace stepped back and looked at him. "What happened to you? Last night you were . . . and now . . . No caffeine for you. At least not till you are home." She sent a text to her husband.

Connan grabbed her hand and pulled her gently to sit beside him. She wrapped her arms around his shoulders and he leaned on her. "You . . . you're the first person to . . ." He turned toward her so he could look at her. "I have never heard the words you said to me my entire life . . . I've never been told that I was lo . . ." He choked up and his voice began to crack. He leaned into her again and wrapped his arms around her waist.

Tears escaped Grace's eyes. "Never?" Connan shook his head but didn't say anything. "Oh, honey," She cried. "I will always love you! Never forget that." She started to rock back and forth with him in her arms. "I'll always love you. You are my son, and you will never go to sleep under my roof without hearing those words!"

Doctor Long opened the door about forty-five minutes later. "Mrs. Rigby, did you have your husband bring you food? If it's for Connan, I'll be confiscating the coffee. He doesn't need caffeine at the present time."

"The coffee is mine," Grace laughed. "I told him no caffeine till he's home. He has the orange juice."

"Alright . . ." Doctor Long looked suspiciously toward Connan.

Connan ignored him. He didn't like shrinks; they always made him feel like something was wrong with him. That was a familiar feeling that he tried to push away. *Wrong move, kid!* Connan's mind exploded, and he almost fell off the bed in a panic. He was shaking uncontrollably. "What's happening to me!" He shouted as Doctor Long ran to his side. "Did you hear that! He's still alive! He's going to kill me!"

Grace was on his other side holding his hand. "He can't hurt you! You're safe, baby!" She looked at Doctor Long almost in a panic herself. "What happened? He was doing so well?!"

"He's having a panic attack." Doctor Long called for a nurse to bring a dose of Valium to calm him down. "I have yet to see this happen, but I thought it might. He's developing PTSD."

Connan tried to hold onto Grace to stop the tremors, but nothing could stop it. Doctor Long stabbed a needle into Connan's arm and injected the medication. A few minutes passed before the tremors slowed and Connan regained a bit of sanity. He gasped for breath.

"He's . . . he's not here!" Connan looked around the room frantically. "He's . . . he's dead. He can't . . . ."

"You're okay, I'm right here, baby." Grace hugged him tight to her chest. "I'm here!"

18

"CONNAN! GOOD TO see you're doing better!" Doctor Long stood up to greet him. "The last three days, you've made leaps and bounds toward recovery!"

"Doc." Connan really didn't want to talk to him.

Doctor Long pretended not to notice the disdain in Connan's voice. "If all goes well, you could be out of here by tomorrow morning if not in a few hours."

Connan sat down opposite the doctor. "I would love to get out of here."

Doctor Long raised an eyebrow. "No, 'I would love to go home'? Is there a reason behind that statement?"

"Well, I have two homes, so I used a more ambiguous term."

Doctor Long laughed. "Ambiguous, huh? Never, in all my years have I heard someone your age say *ambiguous*."

Connan shrugged his shoulders. "I attend a very good boarding school that doesn't allow anyone to slack off . . . even in vocabulary."

"I only have a few things to ask, Connan, so can you hold out a bit longer? I know you don't like me, but can we pretend to get along?"

"I guess, but I don't think answering your questions will help anything. If you can't answer mine, then how is any of this going to help me?"

"I am here to help . . ." The doctor studied him. "You think I can't answer your questions?" The doctor put his notebook aside and leaned forward. "What kind of questions can I not answer?"

Connan looked at him as if deciding whether to actually ask his questions. He looked away and sighed. "No shrink has ever been able to answer my questions . . . Only a preacher or pastor could. Whatever they call religious leaders . . . Cap could probably tell me."

"Ah," Doctor Long nodded his understanding. "Try me?" He took out a voice recorder and stopped it from recording their conversation. "Now, the people who don't wish me to delve into the spiritual realm can't say anything. I'll see what I can answer for you."

Connan's eyebrows were raised. "Why would Dean try and save me? What did he mean to 'have Jesus in my heart'? Why would I even need Him? How could He possibly know anything about my life and what's going on? If He is some powerful being why didn't He prevent any of this from happening?"

"Slow down, Connan." Doctor Long thought for a moment. "You see Dean as your brother, correct?"

"Yeah."

"I know he sees you the same . . . Do you think his love for you isn't real?"

"I don't know, I guess it's real," Connan replied.

"You would do anything to protect him and he would do the same for you. He wasn't giving up on you just as Grace never gave up on you. They love you." The doctor paused. "*Having Jesus in your heart* means to confess Him as your Lord and Savior, as the one and only Son of God, and repent or turn away from your sins." He leaned back in his chair. "God is the creator of the universe. Just as this building was created by an architect, the world was created by God. The Bible says that He, our creator, knit us together in our mother's womb and that He knew us before we were ever conceived."

"So, does that mean He's seen everything I've ever done? Even the times I snuck out in the middle of the night and no one ever knew? The times I kept my friends from getting in trouble so I took the fall instead knowing Dad could just have my record wiped? When I smoked weed and had to crash with Thursday and mom? He's seen the times I spied on my mom and took pictures of her with her boyfriends?"

"Boyfriends?" Doctor Long looked dumbfounded. "No wonder current events have been hard on you, but yes, He's seen it all. Jesus came to earth and chose to die for the sins of the world so that we could inherit eternal life."

"I . . ." Connan stared at the floor. "I don't even know who Jesus is . . . How could He die for me and I do not know who He is?"

Doctor Long stood up and went to his bookshelf. "If you truly want to learn about Jesus then I can let you borrow this." He pulled a small book out of its place and handed it to Connan. "Start with the book of John. It's a firsthand account of Jesus and who He is. Don't tell anyone in this hospital that I hand out Bibles instead of prescriptions."

Connan nodded and turned the Bible over in his hands. "Never had one of these before . . . I've snuck a few moments in Captain Rigby's, but never really understood it . . . ."

Doctor Long tore a corner off a piece of paper in his notebook. "Here, I'll mark John for you, so you don't have to search for it . . . I think you are ready to go home. I'll let Captain Rigby know and then get your discharge papers ready. You can hang out here till I get back."

"You didn't even ask your questions?" Connan looked up at him.

"I didn't need to. Connan, your questions tell me you aren't going to try and harm yourself. They tell me you may be lost but you are searching for answers, not a way out. You aren't a danger to yourself or to others. That's all I needed to write in my report."

Connan slowly nodded then turned the Bible over in his hands. "What about the panic attacks? I've had two over the last few days . . . Will they go away?"

Doctor Long walked to the door of his office. "They may, in time, but PTSD can be triggered by anything . . . I can't promise they will go away, but if you work hard at it, you may be able to control your movements better when they do come."

Connan nodded again and opened the marked page in the Bible. "I'll put it back when Cap gets here. I can borrow his."

Doctor Long left his office after calling Captain Rigby. An hour later, Connan was discharged and on his way back to the Rigbys' house.

"Thank you," Connan said after a long silence. "I don't think I've thanked you for coming for us." He looked out the window. It felt good to be out of the hospital.

"You're welcome, son." John smiled. "No one knows you were released yet, so this is going to be a huge surprise."

Connan smiled. "I can't wait to see them!"

"They have been very anxious and worried about you." John paused. "I've been worried about you."

Connan looked at him. He could see the glimmer of tears in the man's eyes. "Do you think I could go to church with you on Sunday?"

John's voice started to crack. "The invitation has always been there, Connan. I didn't want to force it on you . . . You sure you want to go?"

Connan nodded. "I want what you have . . . what Mom has." Connan tried to explain. "Not that I'm jealous or anything like that, but I want to love the way you do . . . You did everything you could to get to us . . . You weren't going to let us die. Mom saved my life . . . I was going to kill myself the night she showed up at the hospital. If she hadn't been there, I would've succeeded."

"I love you boys very much." John couldn't say any more. He blinked back the tears. They pulled in the driveway. "I'd do anything for my family . . . as long as it's legal."

James was out in the yard throwing a ball to Bailey. They stopped as John pulled up in front of the house. Bailey sniffed the air as John climbed out. He began to whine and ran up to the passenger side door. He jumped on the door and started scratching at the window.

"Bailey! Get off the car!" John shouted. "He can't get out with you on the door!" he pulled at the dog's collar. Once Connan was out, John let go and watched as the dog almost knocked Connan over.

James ran to the door of the house. "Connan's home! Connan's home!"

The house erupted into chaos as everyone tried to rush out the door at the same time. Dean made it out first and tackled him to the ground. Derek followed and dove on top of his twin. They lay there laughing together until Troy came and tried to jump on Connan. Tracy and Grace laughed at the boys from the porch. Bailey wagged his entire backside as he clambered over the boys trying to lick Connan's face.

"What a surprise! I thought Doctor Long would keep you at least another day or two!" Grace was almost jumping up and down with excitement. Connan jumped onto the porch skipping the stairs all together. He wrapped Grace into a hug.

"I thought so too!" He didn't want to let go. "I love you, Mom."

"I love you so much!" She pushed Connan away and cupped his cheeks in her hands. "Welcome home!"

"My turn!" Tracy rushed him and grabbed him around the waist. "I'm so glad you're home!"

Connan wrapped his arms around her shoulders. "I'm glad to be home too!" They half pushed him into the house. They all wanted to talk to him and be close to him the rest of the night. Dean reserved the right to sit next to him at the dinner table. Grace had made lasagna for supper. He loved her food. Especially the lasagna. Connan closed his eyes and tried to follow along with the blessing of the food this time. He had never done so before.

"Way, way better than hospital food!" Connan wiped his mouth with a napkin. He could think of no other place he'd rather be than at the dinner table with his adopted family. He sat back and put his hands behind his head. He closed his eyes. *I want to stay here forever! And to think, I couldn't stand this part of the day when I first got here!* After a minute or two, he nudged Dean's arm. "You two want to play some brawl?"

"Yes!" Derek jumped out of his seat. "I call dibs on Plato!" The table went silent. Everyone turned to Derek, wide-eyed.

"Derek!" Connan stood. "When did you start . . . ?"

"After you were taken . . ." Derek blushed. He took his plate to the sink. "I figured there was no point in staying silent . . . I wanted to say all I wanted to say to you before if you came back to us!"

Connan found it hard to speak. He grabbed his plate and took it to the sink as well. After a minute he said, "If you get Plato then I get Medrid!"

"I call Reaper!" Dean followed Connan to the sink. "And no cheating, Connan!"

"I never cheat!" Connan laughed. "I'm just that good! Gonna have to get better if you want to beat me!" As Connan passed the table, he bent down and gave Grace a kiss on the cheek. "Supper was great, Mom. Thanks!"

"I wanna play!" James tried to hurry and finish eating. "Wait for me!"

"Oh," Connan turned around. "Congrats, Tracy! I knew you could do it!" He backed toward the stairs leading to the second floor. "Care to join us?"

Tracy's eyes lit up. "As long as Dean doesn't hog the controller!"

"If he does, you can take a turn with mine!" Connan turned and took the stairs two at a time. Only once the clock struck midnight did John call all of them to go to bed.

"Night, guys," Connan said with a yawn. He retraced his steps down the stairs. Grace had just crossed the living room with John. Connan opened the door to his room. "Night, Mom; night, Dad. Love you!" He closed the door before either could react.

"Do you think he will be alright when he sees his dad?" Grace whispered.

John stared at his door. "It's hard to tell . . . It could trigger panic, anger, betrayal. We should ask Doctor Long what he thinks . . . He will see him next week no matter what."

The next morning, Connan woke early and put on a pair of running shorts. He ran up the stairs and knocked on Tracy's door. To his surprise she opened it and was dressed for a run. He smiled. "Was going to see if you wanted to run, but it looks like you do!"

She hugged him. "I'm so glad you're back!" She let go and he followed her back downstairs. Grace greeted them at the bottom of the stairs.

"Going somewhere?" she asked.

"For a quick run, if that's okay." Tracy bounced on her toes. "Just a couple miles!"

"One," Grace replied.

"One and a half?" Connan negotiated.

Grace squinted at him. "One and a quarter and no farther. Dad's bringing us breakfast from BJ's."

"Sweet! Donuts for breakfast!" Connan rubbed his hands together. "We'll be back in a flash!" The two teens headed to the door. They took a ten-minute run then returned and showered as fast as possible. By the time they had done all this, John was walking in with a large paper bag that had *"BJ's Donuts"* on the side.

"I'm starved!" Tracy peeked in the top of the bag.

"What, no morning bathroom routine?" John teased.

"No, Connan and I have already ran over a mile and just finished showers! Mom said you were bringing breakfast!"

"So, you drag him out as soon as he gets home . . ." John shook his head. "Did you at least want to go?" He gave Connan an inquisitive look.

"Yeah! I went to go see if she wanted to run. I've missed our routine the last few weeks."

"Grab some food and come outside for a minute." John held the bag up. "I'd like to talk to you about something."

"Okay . . ." Connan grabbed a plate from the cabinet. He overheard Grace ask, "Are you going to tell him?"

"Doctor Long says we should, but he said he will be present in case Connan goes into a fit." John kissed his wife and stepped out on the porch.

Connan grabbed a couple donuts and headed for the door. *Must not be too bad if I can eat and talk . . . the part about Doc being present is a bit weird.* He closed the door behind him then sat down next to John on the stairs. "So, what's up? This isn't about me using your Bible, is it?" Connan took a bite of a cinnamon sugar twist donut.

"I knew it was you," John got serious. "No, I want to talk to you about your dad." John stated. "He's in town."

"I've kind of been wondering when he was going to show up . . . Don't think I could handle seeing him at this point." Connan replied. "I'd probably try and knock some of his teeth loose or go into a panic fit."

"He's not allowed to see you till next Friday." John looked at him in all seriousness. "I'm going to ask you to try not to react when you do see him. It may hurt what we are trying to do."

Connan swallowed. "And what exactly are you trying to do?"

"Connan, it's only been a week and a half since Daryn almost killed you. Your dad wasn't coming. Once you had to be taken to the hospital for severe shock, I had Grace contact our lawyer." He took a deep breath. "Connan, we're trying to keep you from having to go back to Denver."

Connan choked on a piece of donut he had just placed in his mouth. "What? Really?"

"Yes," John said. He stopped Connan from taking another bite. "We can legally fight for you to stay if we charge him with neglect. In your case, it's very possible we could win. Your dad is fighting us though."

"He was going to let me die . . . I . . . I don't want to go back." Connan put his plate aside. "I'll run away if I have to. I'm not going anywhere with him."

"We can make a medical plea." John gave him a stern look. "There will be no running away. Doctor Long doesn't think it wise to put you in the same room with your dad. He thinks it could trigger your PTSD. He's going to be present in case that does happen. We've already notified the judge and so has the doctor. He's going to fit you with a portable heart monitor so he can see any irregular spikes. That way we can prevent an attack or at least get you out of there before it gets too bad to move you."

Connan looked out toward the animal pins. "Do you think we have a chance?"

"Yes."

Connan's eyes began to water. "I still don't understand why you would fight for me like this . . . You've only known me a couple of months now . . . Why . . . ?"

"We love you, Connan." John didn't hesitate. "I believe God brought you to us that night you laid your bike over. Everything fell into place. Your cover was a foster child. Grace and I have four foster children. One more wouldn't raise alerts anywhere. God knew you needed us as much as we needed you. You helped break the barriers with Derek and have been a very protective big brother to Tracy. Troy and James adore you, Connan. And Dean ... I never thought he would get close to anyone other than his twin and Grace. He's broken out of his shell too. You have never had constant parental guidance and that's something we are able to give you."

Connan held back the tears. "There has to be a God! There has to be! No one has ever fought for me like you do! I'd never heard the words '*I love you*' till Grace walked in on the night I was going to kill myself! I've taken the fall every time ... Here ... I'm actually cared about and loved! I'll do anything it takes to stay! Just tell me what I need to do!"

John smiled and wrapped an arm around Connan's shoulders. "All you have to do is sit quietly in the courtroom and not punch your dad."

"Is the entire family going to be there?"

"Grace and the twins will be. Tracy said she'd watch the younger two since they can't sit still. She doesn't want to be there if the judge denies our request."

"In that case," Connan replied. "If Mom is in the room, I'll probably have a lot more self-control . . . If I don't have to look at him, I should be fine." He laughed. "I can't believe I have a chance to stay here!"

John squeezed his shoulders and pulled him into a side hug. "We want you to stay too."

19

CONNAN SAT ON the floor with Dean and Derek on either side of him. They sat outside the Family Court that had been assigned their case. Doctor Long had been waiting on them. He had brought a nurse with him and informed Connan he would be getting vitals before entering the courtroom. It was almost ten o'clock.

"Connan, stop fidgeting." John had his arms crossed and stood in front of him. "It's not going to help anything."

"Sorry." Connan shook his head. "I'm just really nervous." He stopped shaking his foot.

"We all are." John looked at his lawyer. "How much longer before we go in?"

"Should be any minute." Lawyer Eldree said. He scratched his dark chin. His voice was deep and smooth. He reminded Connan of a talk show host.

A clerk opened the door to the courtroom. "We're ready for you. Eldree, you, Captain Rigby, and Mr. Hyatt will go up front. The rest of you will sit behind them."

"Connan, vitals before you go in." Doctor Long beckoned him over. "I also want to check your monitor."

The clerk looked concerned. "I will tell the judge you will be in in a moment."

"He has not seen his dad and I believe it could trigger an attack." Doctor Long placed a blood pressure cuff on Connan's arm. "We'll be, just a second; just taking every precaution we can." He took down Connan's vitals and made sure the heart monitor was recording the same heart rate as he was. "Just try not to look at him. If you start to shake or feel odd in any way, get my attention. The monitor should pick it up as well since your heart rate will spike." Connan nodded.

Everyone took their seats while Connan got his vitals taken. Once he and Eldree were in place, the courtroom officer called, "All rise." They stood as the judge came in and took his seat.

Eldree stayed standing after the judge had sat down. He addressed the room. "Your Honor, Captain Rigby and his wife are asking for full guardianship of Connan Hyatt. Connan has been staying in the Rigbys' home under cover as one of their foster children. He was running from a man named Daryn Moroe who was hunting his father. After recent events, Captain Rigby has brought two charges against Mr. Hyatt. The first being neglect and the second, reckless endangerment of a miner."

"I have read over the case file, Mr. Eldree," The judge replied. "You may continue."

Connan thought all was going well. He didn't even try to look at his dad. He felt angry, but something else kept butting into his mind. Daryn's words started to reverberate through his thoughts. "He's not coming . . . I'm sorry, Connan . . . ."

"Mr. Hyatt?" Eldree nudged Connan. Connan jumped in response to Eldree then looked up at the attorney who had spoken. "Would you please take the stand?"

Connan slowly stood up and walked to the judge's left side. Doctor Long watched him closely. His assistant tapped him on the shoulder and showed him Connan's heart rhythm. It had started to spike. A deputy approached Connan and had him place his left hand on the Bible then raise his right hand. "Do you solemnly swear to tell the truth, the whole truth, and nothing but the truth, so help you God?"

"I . . . I do." Connan sat down. He took a quick second to look over at his dad. He had a blank look on his face. Connan did not like it. He didn't look at the attorney. Visions from the warehouse incident raced through his head. *Nice try, but you'll have to do better than that! He's not coming, is he? I thought for sure your dad would protect you at any cost! He's not coming!* Connan was shaking. Doctor Long stood suddenly and tapped Eldree on the shoulder and showed him what he was seeing. *Wrong move, kid.* Connan's breathing became labored as the sound of a gunshot reverberated through his head. He jerked and fell out of the chair.

"Your Honor, my client needs medical attention!" Eldree approached the bench and tried to move Connan, but he was shaking too much to move him. He curled into a ball as he had after Dean had pushed him to the ground in the warehouse.

"Doctor, tend to your patient. If he cannot recover, then we will reconvene at a later time." The judge was on his feet, watching Connan.

Connan couldn't control the shaking. Doctor Long took a syringe from his medical bag and flicked it. "I told you it was a mistake to put him in the same room with Mr. Hyatt." He fumed. "I knew it would trigger him!" He pushed the needle into Connan's arm. "This is a low dose of Valium, Your Honor. If he doesn't recover, I will need to remove him from the courtroom altogether; if not, call an ambulance to come pick us up."

"We will wait to see if he can recover. We will need his statement as to what happened in the warehouse that has triggered these episodes." The judge looked concerned as Connan continued to shake.

"Doctor!" The nurse picked up the small monitor. "His heart!"

"Let's get him out of here! John, call a medic, I don't have the medication I need!" Doctor Long picked Connan up as if he were no more than a child.

"Can't you see this is all a fake out!" Mr. Norries approached the bench. "They are all trying to make my client look like a terrible father!"

"Mr. Norries, if I don't take him to a medic, he will have a heart attack!" Doctor Long shouted as he reached the door with his assistant and Connan. "If he doesn't get what he needs, he could die!"

Eldree turned toward the judge. "His client left Connan to take the fall for him. Mr. Rigby's foster son, Dean, would be able to give his testimony as to what happened at a further date. Connan is no longer stable. Dean was with Connan in the warehouse. Daryn ended up taking him in order to control Connan. By the rhythm on the monitor, he will need to go to the ER if the medic can't slow his heart."

"My client was too far away to get to him in time. You know that, Eldree," Mr. Norries argued. "He was halfway around the world!"

"In that case, if you want to use that excuse, he neglected the boy by leaving him to fend for himself! I have several calls over the last few weeks that show the Rigbys' attempts to get a hold of Mr. Hyatt, but he refused to even answer his son's calls. If he cared at all about his son's safety, he would have never left the States in the first place!"

"You expect my client to just hand over his rights to his own son because he was halfway around the world? He just found out his wife's been cheating on him, and you want to devastate him more?

Eldree raised his voice at Norries. "His mother should've been charged with neglect long ago! She pretends the boy doesn't even exist!"

"Order!" The judge banged his gavel on the desk. "As the witness had to be rushed out, Mr. Rigby's boy may take the stand. Is that agreeable, Mr. Norries?"

The attorney nodded. "I guess it will have to do."

"Good, we will reconvene later today at two o'clock without him present." The judge banged his gavel again.

Connan was still shaking violently when John, Grace, and the boys followed them out. A medic ran up the stairs with a narcotic case. "Here, Doc. This should do the trick. Shouldn't have any negative effects with the Valium dose."

Doctor Long had the medic help him find a vein and keep Connan's arm still enough to inject the drug. "Thank you. Is your partner coming? I want to take him to the ER and put him on a 12 lead for a bit. I'd rather be at the hospital if he does have a reaction. Or, if his heart doesn't slow." He checked the monitor his assistant carried. "It's still pretty chaotic, but it will take a few for the drugs to set in."

"Is he okay?" John asked.

"His blood pressure skyrocketed when he couldn't avoid seeing Mr. Hyatt." Doctor Long was still fuming. "He should've never been called to the stand. He could easily have a heart attack with this high of a rhythm."

"Does he need to go to the hospital?" Grace asked. She knelt by Connan's side and took his hand in hers. "It's okay, you're okay . . . ."

"I think it's best; just for an hour or two. Then we can take him home. That way he's in a familiar place that is safe when he wakes up. This stuff will knock him out for a few hours at least. His body will be exhausted. If you don't mind company, we will stick around till after he wakes to make sure there were no complications."

John looked furious but kept his calm. "Grace, can you and Derek take him home? Dean and I will stay and testify later on. Doctor Long, it would be most appreciated if your assistant could go with them. You may need to come back and testify as you saw his state in the hospital."

"What time do I need to be back? I'll make sure to bring printouts of Connan's heart record for the past ten minutes." Doctor Long stepped back as the medic's EMT arrived with the cot. "As long as nothing goes wrong, we should only be in the ER for about an hour."

"The judge said we would reconvene at two. Dean will testify on his behalf." After the doctor agreed, John poked his head inside the courtroom and motioned for Eldree to come to the door. "He has to go to the ER. Doctor Long will be back to testify and will be sending his assistant with Grace to help her get him comfortable once they are out of the hospital."

Two o'clock rolled around slowly. The doctor had showed up around one saying Connan was recovering well and he had sent him home with his assistant and Grace. Once they were settled into their seats again, Doctor Long was called to the stand; after a brief report of Connan's condition and his stay in the psychiatric wing, Captain Rigby took the stand, then Dean. Dean was sworn in by a deputy then sat down. He crossed his arms over his chest.

"State your name for the court, please." Mr. Norries said.

"Dean Malcolm Perry, soon to be Rigby." Dean stated in a matter-of-fact way.

"How old are you?"

"Thirteen," he replied again.

"How long have you known Connan?" The attorney asked.

"Since June sometime," Dean answered.

"And what happened in the warehouse that has made Connan have these attacks?"

Dean glared at Todd. "He gave up. After he found out that HE wasn't coming to save him," he pointed at Mr. Hyatt. "He didn't want to live anymore. Connan gave up . . . He had no hope of rescue from him. He told me he wanted to die; that he had no family."

"Why would Connan be afraid of his dad?" Mr. Norries asked him.

"He's not afraid of his dad, it's all because his dad left him to die!" Dean jumped out of his seat. He looked straight at Todd. "You left him to die! How could you? You don't care about him; I don't think you even love him! What kind of father makes his kid take the fall for him?" Dean sat down in a huff. He calmed himself. "Sorry, Your Honor, I shouldn't have yelled at Mr. Hyatt, but he really hurt Connan, so much so the doctor had to take him away again." He sniffed and wiped away a few stray tears.

"You can step down, son." The judge asked if there were any more testimonies. Todd never once spoke aloud. Dean's outburst had caught him off guard. Eldree was telling the judge there were no more witnesses when Mr. Norries stood.

"Your Honor, my client does not wish to drag this out. He has decided to turn over his rights. He does not wish his son any more harm than what has already occurred."

The judge looked at him over his spectacles. "Is this true, Mr. Hyatt? Once you sign over guardianship, it cannot be undone."

Todd stood and addressed the Judge. "Yes, Your Honor. He was in a lot of distress over the incident with Moroe. I do not want to cause him any more harm than I already have. He is safer here and I can tell by Mr. Perry's testimony that he is very much loved . . . Something I have neglected to give him myself."

20

CONNAN BOLTED UPRIGHT in his bed. He looked around frantically. Bailey stood up from where he was lying next to him and started licking him in the face. He stroked the dog's fur. *I'm fine. No one can hurt me. Was that all a dream?* He lowered his feet off the side of the bed and stood up. He could hear the indistinct voices of adults in the living room. The sun was still pretty high in the sky, so he didn't think he had slept too terribly long. His alarm clock said three twenty-five. *Did I pass out in the courtroom?* He looked at his hands. He wasn't shaking. Other than a dull pain in his chest and feeling exhausted, he thought the worst had passed. *I feel terrible . . . I wonder how bad it was . . . I don't think I've ever had an episode that extreme.*

Bailey sat on the bed watching him. "I bet you're happy I'm home." He watched as the dog began panting. Bailey looked as if he were smiling. Connan went around to the door and opened it. "Want to go outside?" Bailey jumped off the bed and followed him out the door. Doctor Long sat on the sectional talking with John. The nurse that had been with him at the courthouse was there too. Connan rubbed the grogginess from his eyes and pressed a hand against his chest trying to push the annoying pain out.

John jumped up from his usual seat in the corner. "How are you feeling?"

"Like I got ran over by a train." Connan rubbed his eyes again. "Did I pass out in the courtroom? I can't remember anything after taking the stand."

"You had a severe panic attack," John replied. "Doctor Long had to take you to the ER for a couple hours. We thought you were going to have a heart attack at one point." He walked over to him. "You don't remember anything?"

Connan shook his head. "No. I remember having my hand on the Bible and my other one raised, and I looked over at Dad. After that, I'm lost."

"You were removed from the room and Dean was called instead. He may or may not have thrown a tantrum toward your dad. But, long story short, Todd gave us guardianship. You get to stay here."

"What?" Connan whispered. He pushed on his chest again. "I can stay?"

John cleared his throat. "Yes. You're ours now."

Connan felt like his heart had skipped a beat. His eyes watered. "I . . . I'm home?"

John shook his head. "OOF!" Connan almost tackled him to the floor with a hug. Connan pulled away wiping his eyes.

"Thank you . . . I don't know what to say . . ." He couldn't help the happy tears. He laughed. "There has got to be a God!"

"Connan?" Tracy ran down the stairs. "Connan!" She ran to him and gave him a great big hug. "You get to stay!" She kissed his cheek. "I can't believe it! I'm no longer the oldest!" She let go of him and almost skipped into the kitchen.

John looked at her, his voice stern. "This doesn't mean you can slack off on the responsibilities you have, young lady."

Connan laughed. "I'll gladly take some of her load on!" He spread his arms wide. "I have a family! I'm not cleaning her room though. It's messier than the twins' combined!" He ducked as Tracy threw an empty water bottle at him. "Oh! You wanna go?"

"Don't you dare!" Tracy ran to the back side of the island, smiling at him.

Derek came in the front door. "Connan!" He poked his head back outside. "Hey, guys! Connan's awake!"

Connan was still not used to Derek using his voice. "Dude, I am never going to get used to you talking." He laughed again. "I'll never be an only child again!" The dull pain in his chest was forgotten.

The doctor stood. "Well, I can see we aren't really needed here. We'll head on home. Try and get some rest, Connan; you're going to be tired from the drug administration and your heart being in overdrive. Dinner's on me tonight!" He looked at John. "Send me everyone's favorite pizza. I'm buying the house dinner tonight. That way everyone can celebrate the latest member of the Rigby family. Come on, Ryan."

Dean tackled Connan when he got close enough. "That's for freaking out on me!" He had a broad grin plastered on his face. They wrestled back and forth till Connan got him into a headlock he couldn't escape. Dean soon gave up and hung like a rag doll in Connan's grip. "Uncle, uncle!"

Connan thanked the doctor for looking after him during the court hearing. Doctor Long said his goodbyes and he and his assistant left for their own homes. John let the boys bring their gaming console down so they could hold a tournament. The champions came down to Connan and Derek. Pizza arrived around seven.

Connan was up earlier than usual the next morning. He looked in the usual spot and found John's Bible. He found the book of John and opened it where he had left off in Doctor Long's office. He then decided to start over. He decided to take notes, like he would in school. *This way, I can ask questions.* He read for an hour then placed his notes underneath and put it back where it belonged. He put a strip of paper in his spot instead of folding the corner of the page. John always read before bed, so Connan decided to read before his morning runs with Tracy. *If this god truly is a savior, then I want to find out the truth about him!*

A few days later he was called out to the porch by John. He had a box in his hands. "School will be starting soon and I need to know if I need to enroll you here. Are you wanting to attend the boarding school in North Carolina?"

"I talked to Sergeant Tibbens about it yesterday . . . There's no point in me going there anymore."

John gave him a questioning look. "Why not?"

Connan sat down where he always did on the stairs when talking with either of his adopted parents. "The episodes . . . Sarg said I won't be able to join the Marines . . . I would only be a liability. He said they would still love to have me, but I can't join up after I graduate." His disappointment was clear. "It will be quite the experience to go to a public school."

"I'll have Grace get in touch with the school." John pulled a bigger box out of the shadows. "In the meantime, I thought you might like to have this."

Connan eyed the box then looked at Rigby. "What is it?"

"Open it and see." John smiled.

Connan began to open the box. A black shiny surface made him gasp. "No way!" He pulled his bike helmet out. "I get my bike back?"

"You can ride to work with me tomorrow and pick it up. I put a legal plate on it on my last shift. Your dad wanted you to keep it." He handed Connan a smaller box. "I also got you this . . . I think you will find it useful."

This box was wrapped in newspaper and tied with twine. It was small and rectangular in shape. Connan unwrapped it. When he saw the cover, his eyes widened. "My own . . . Dad . . . !"

"Now you can stop marking up mine and mark in your own!" John couldn't help his joy. *Lord, he's a wonderful boy. May he learn from You and Your Word.*

Connan took the leather-bound Bible from the box. He ran his fingers over the cover. "Never thought I'd be this excited over a book!" He flipped through some of the pages. "Is this a study Bible?"

John nodded. "It also has built-in space for notes . . . You can still leave me notes in mine if you have questions."

Connan's smile grew. "Thank you. It's been really great with the reference answers . . . About school . . ." Connan became serious. "How different is public school from military schools?"

"For one," John replied. "No uniforms. Two, kids aren't held to a certain standard, so bullying has been running rampant the last few years . . . Punching bullies is frowned upon by the way."

"So, I should try not to get suspended . . . Frank will be surprised to see me." Connan snorted as he imagined Frank tripping over himself when he first sees him at school. "I'm sure I'll have a military attitude going in . . . I've never been to another type of school."

"The school does have an ROTC program."

"Wouldn't be able to join. They sign the kids up right after graduation, they go straight to basic. Maybe I can join the wrestling team or something."

John shook his head. "I can't see you as a wrestler. They do have a gamer group. You could always try out for track. They will have the boys' tryouts first week of school."

"We'll see." Connan laughed. "Running with Tracy is about all I can take! Though, to make this school feel more like my old one, I may run two miles before school in the mornings." He ran his hands over the Bible again. "My life is about to change forever . . . Jesus was a real human . . . He is also the Son of God, isn't he? . . . I've never read this, but I can tell that's where John is going in his book. He is telling me that Jesus is the Son of God and he got to witness Him in action . . . ."

John pulled him into a side hug. "That's one of the first steps toward giving your life to him. The first step to letting Him be your savior."

"I think He already is." Connan looked at his guardian. "He brought me to you . . . He saved me through you . . . And Mom . . . She said He told her to come to the hospital the day I was going to . . . I know I have a lot to learn, but . . ." He held up his new Bible. "This is where I need to start."

ACKNOWLEDGMENTS

FIRST AND FOREMOST, I thank my Lord and Savior, Jesus Christ. He has given me the ability to create and a passion for writing. He is the reason I create stories. He gave me the desire to write.

Second, I must thank my mother for all her love and support. She's been my

best friend as far back as I can remember, and her love is unconditional. She is my rock and when I need to talk, she's always there. I love this woman dearly and pray she lives a long and happy life.

Third, I must thank my brother for inspiring me, with his character, to write this book. He is a big supporter of my writing career and

I love getting his feedback. He inspires me to write. My characters always have a taste of his personality in them. I also thank my nephew for being a big part of this project. He was one of my first readers of this book and was my insight to the teenage mind. He has been a big help in developing this story.

I would also like to thank my pastor for his insight on pieces of my novel along with my cousin who is also a pastor. They helped me refine some of the pieces that I believed were lacking.

Last, but not least, I must thank two of my friends and my husband. My friends have supported me in my writing and my best friend is partly the reason I was able to come up with the character Grace. She loves her family and is dedicated to them. She works so hard to make all those around her happy. She is a mentor and a beautiful lady all around. I don't know where I'd be without her friendship and support.

My husband, and love of my life, is a big supporter of my pursuit of writing. Though I don't always let him read my books, he loves that I love to write and always supports me. He asks the right questions when I need another perspective to get past my writer's block. I can't imagine life without him.

Thank you to all who support my love of writing and thank you to my

proofreaders who have gotten the first taste of my writing style. I love you all and Thank God for you!

www.ingramcontent.com/pod-product-compliance
Lightning Source LLC
Chambersburg PA
CBHW030232170426
43201CB00006B/187